KATJA PUDOR

Protocols

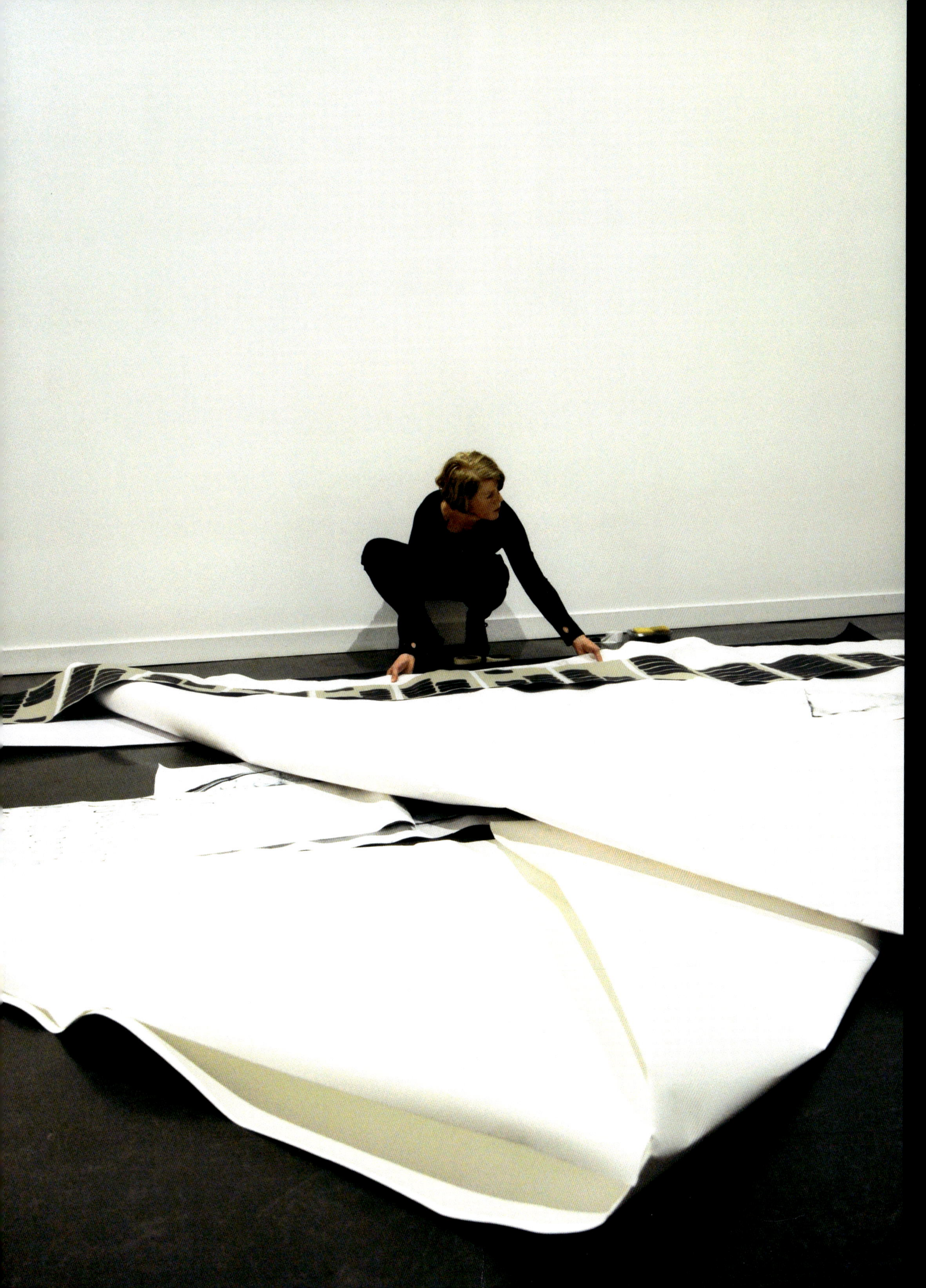

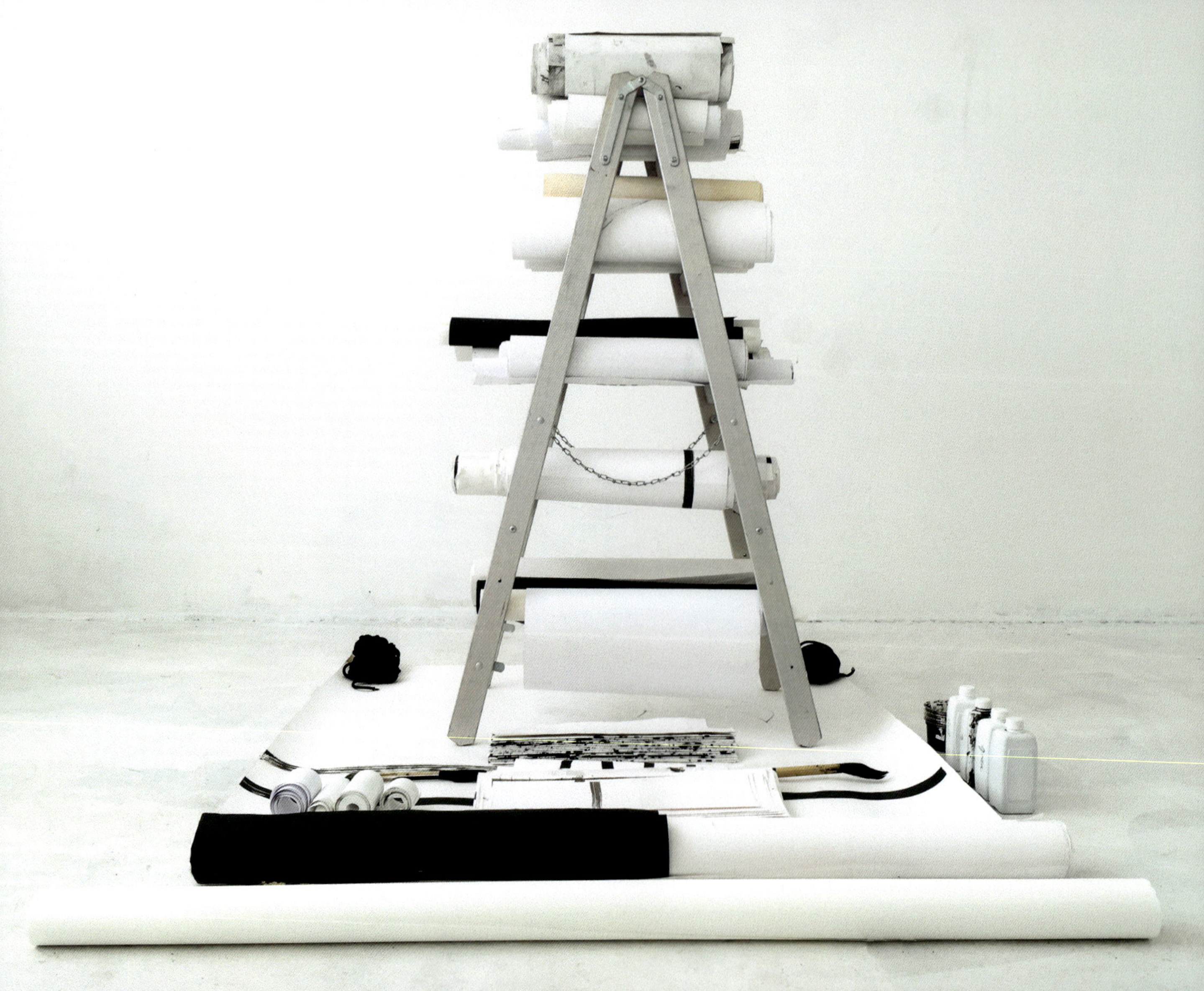

MANIPULATING THE ARCHIVE

Installation, studio view
Different media on various papers
2019

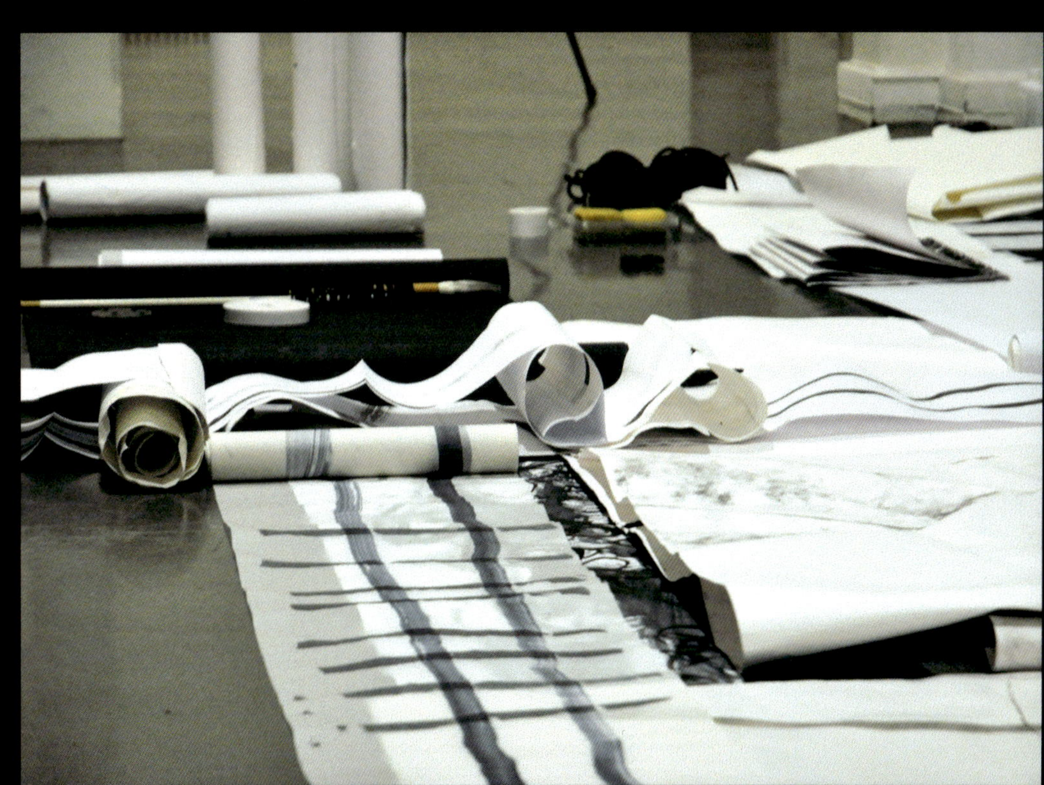

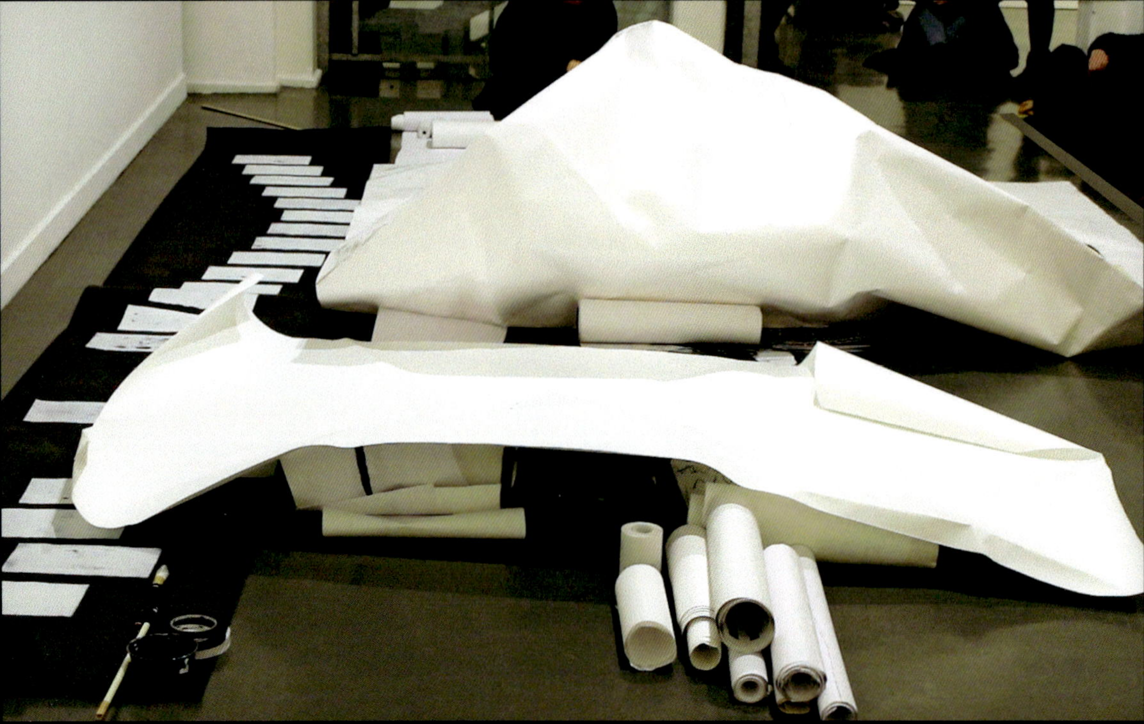

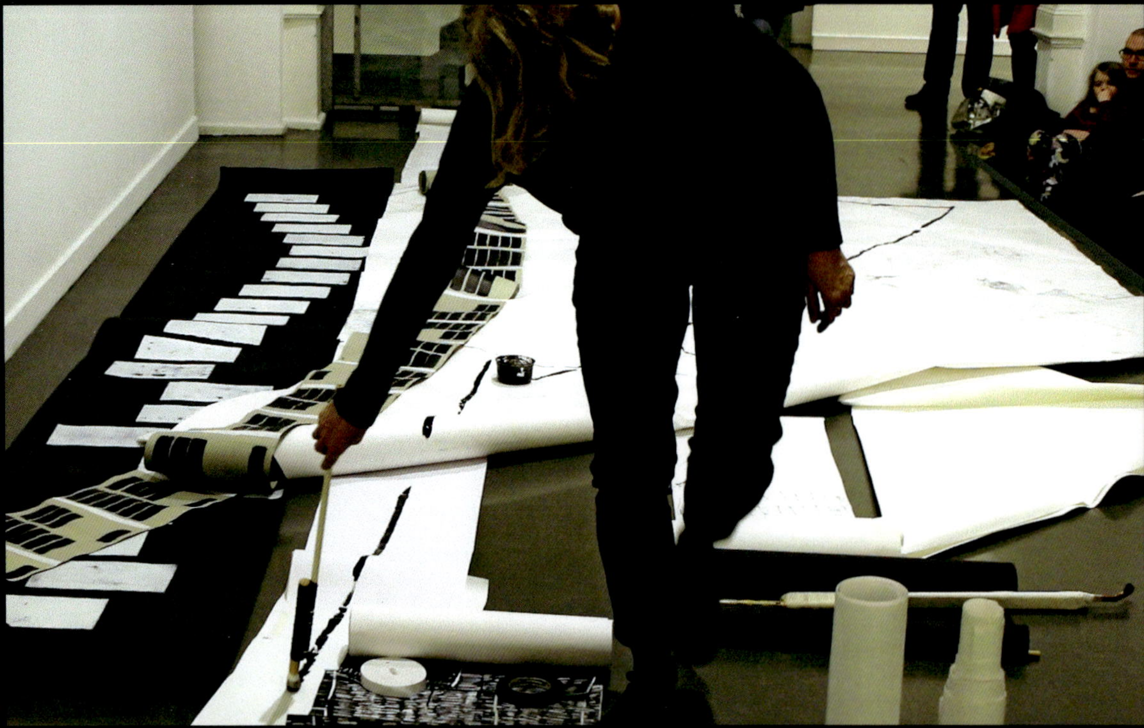

Performance, duration: 30 min
Different media on various papers
Kunstquartier Bethanien / Studio 1, Berlin
Installation and performance as a part
of the group show *the horizon looks different*

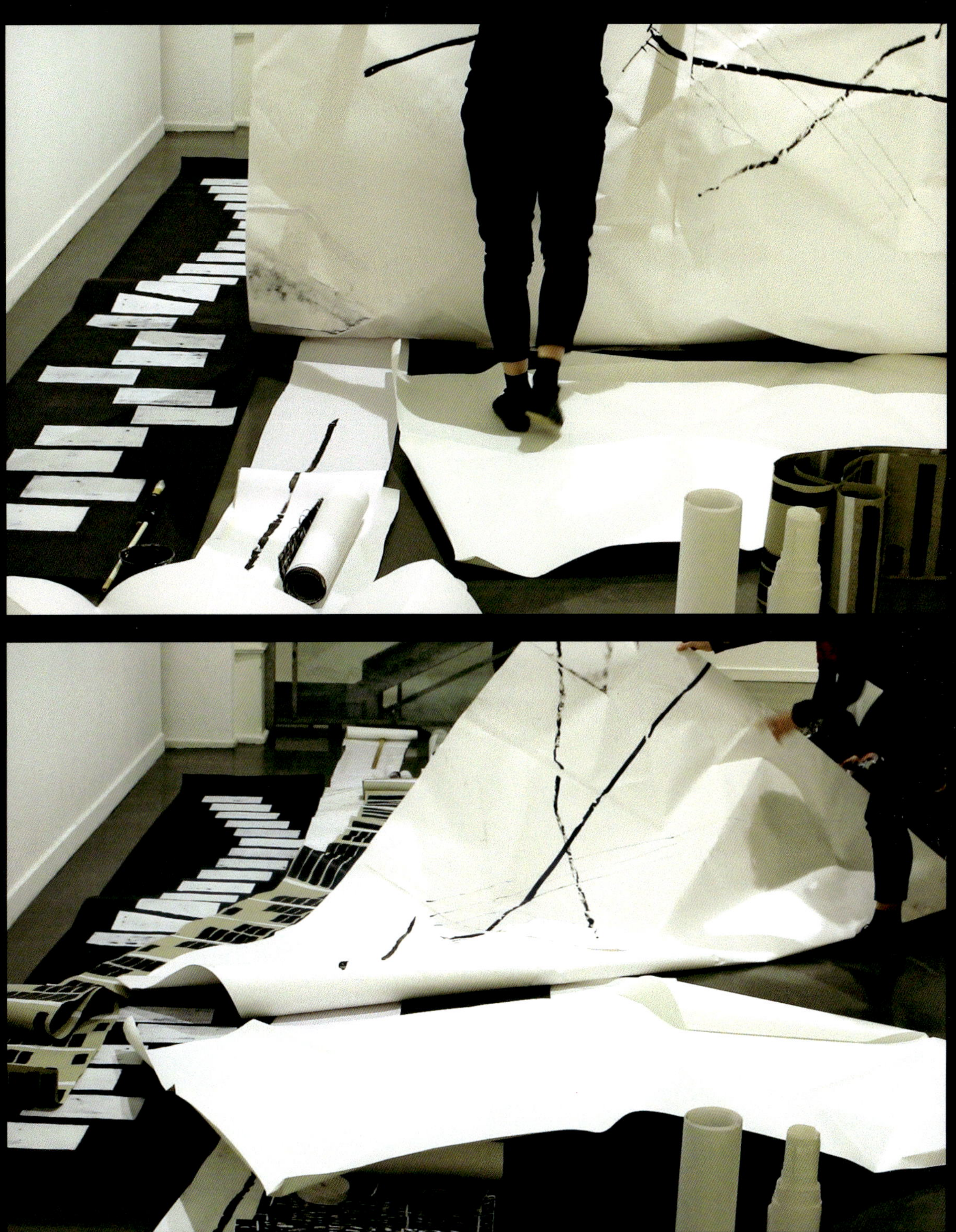

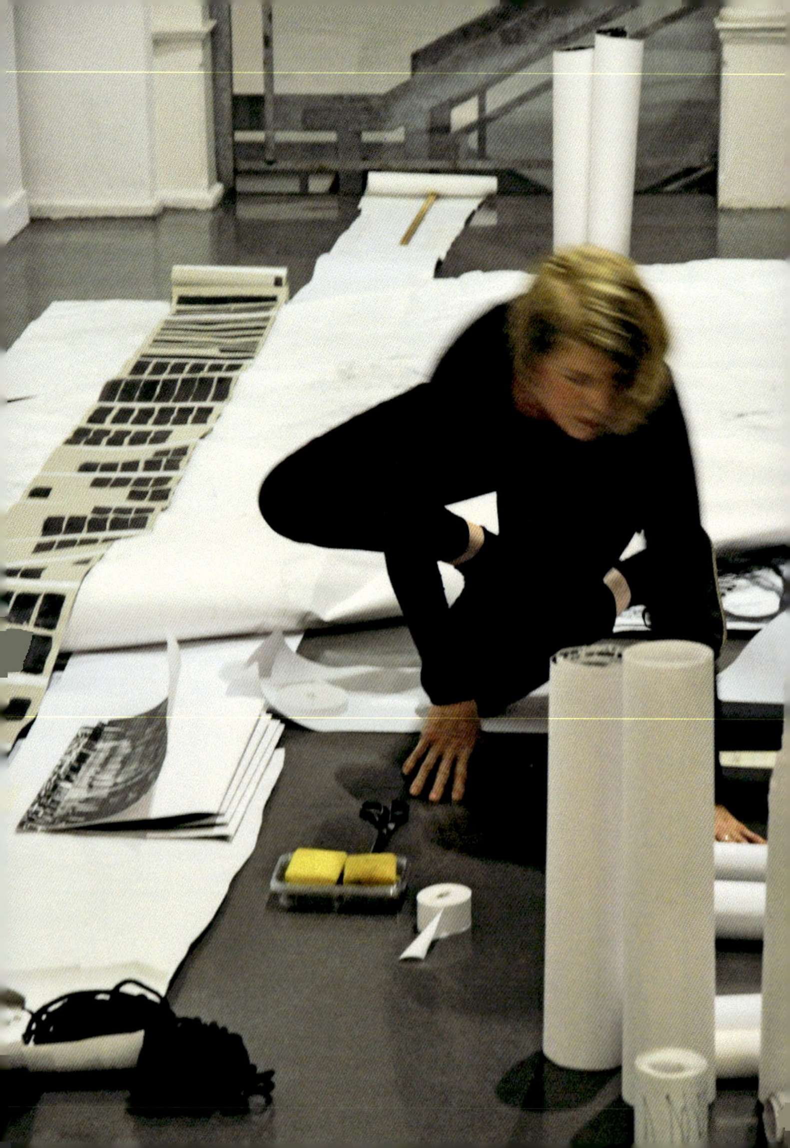

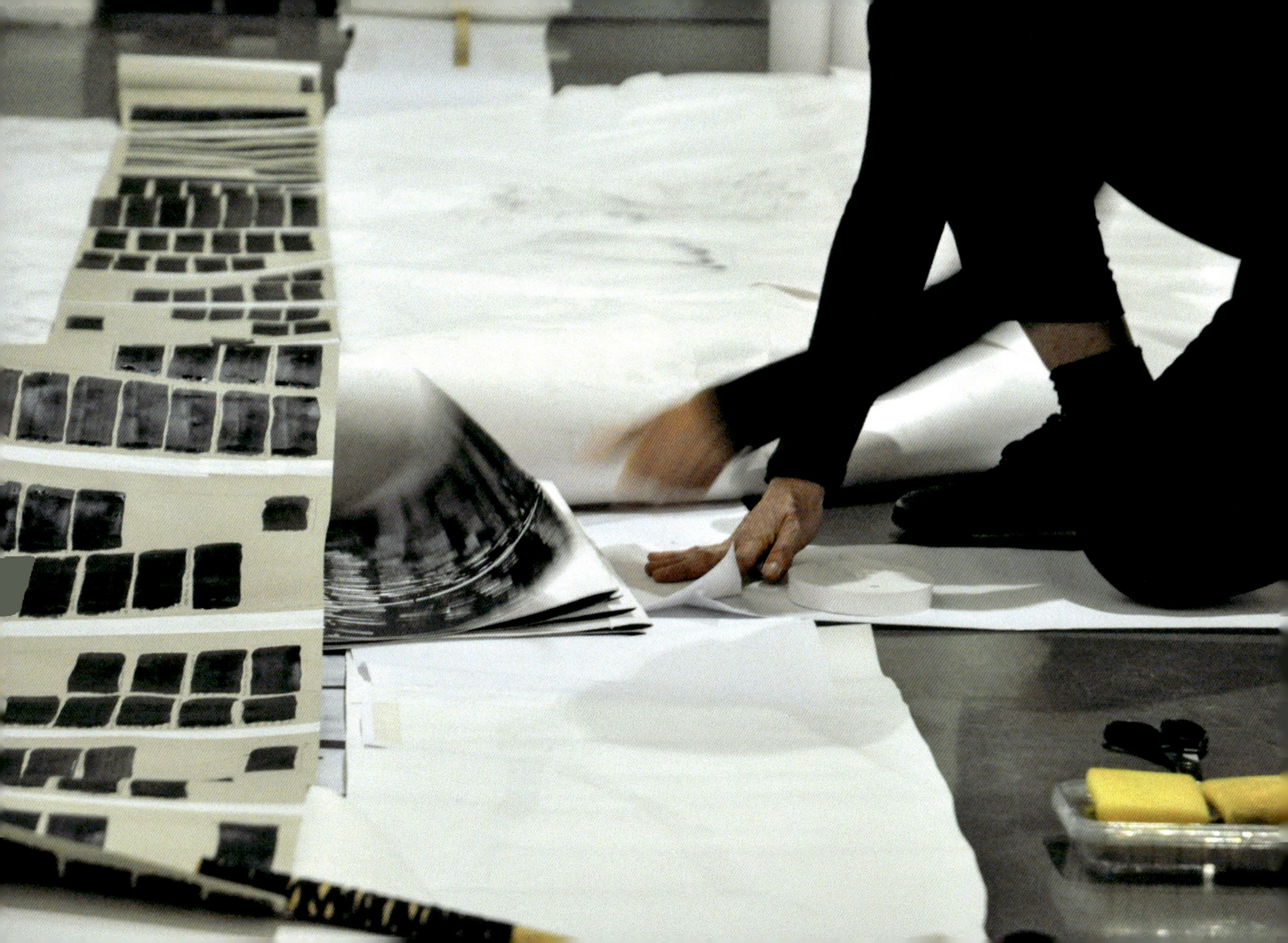

PROTOCOLS OF REMEMBERING

Linocut from multiple
plates on book pages
2019

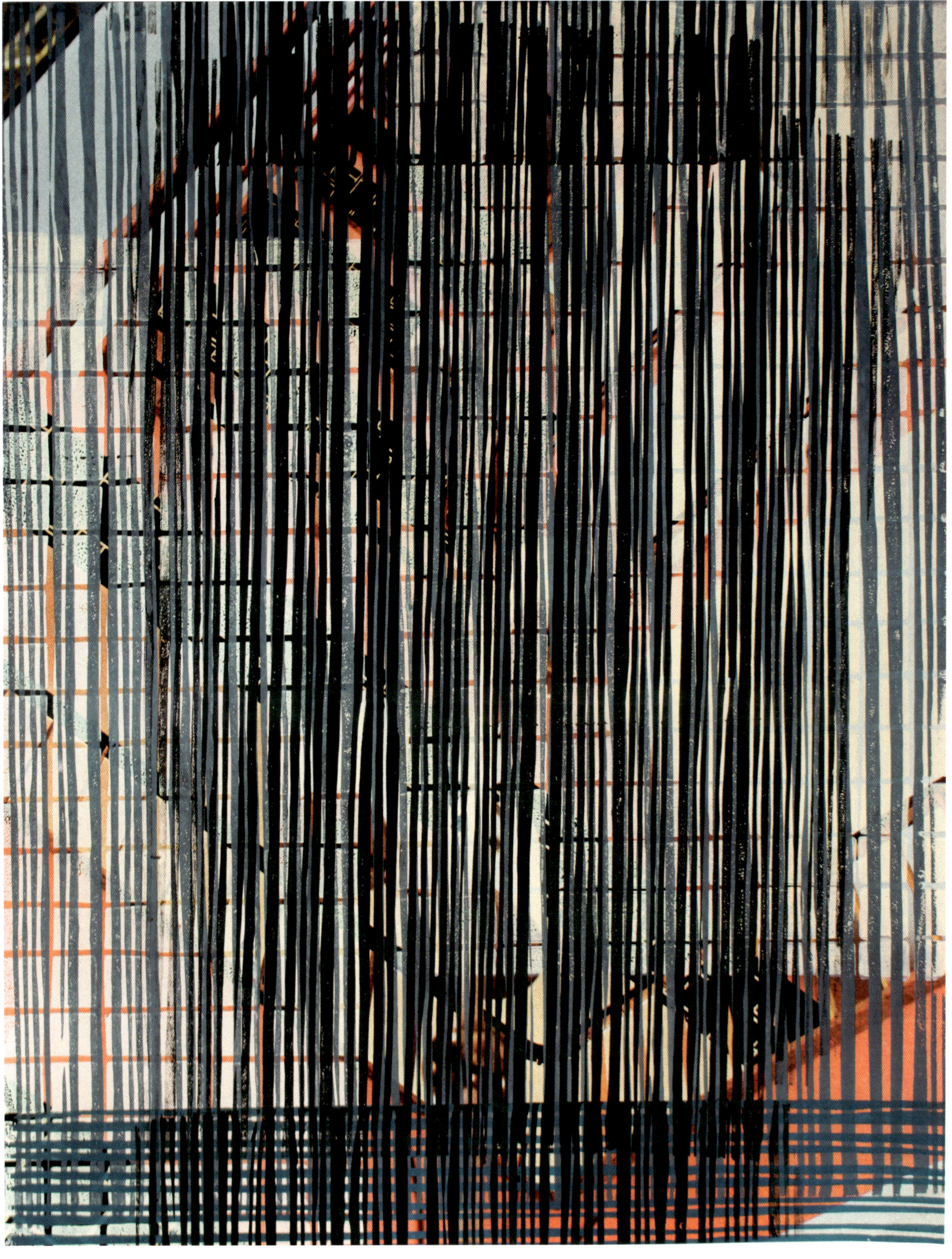

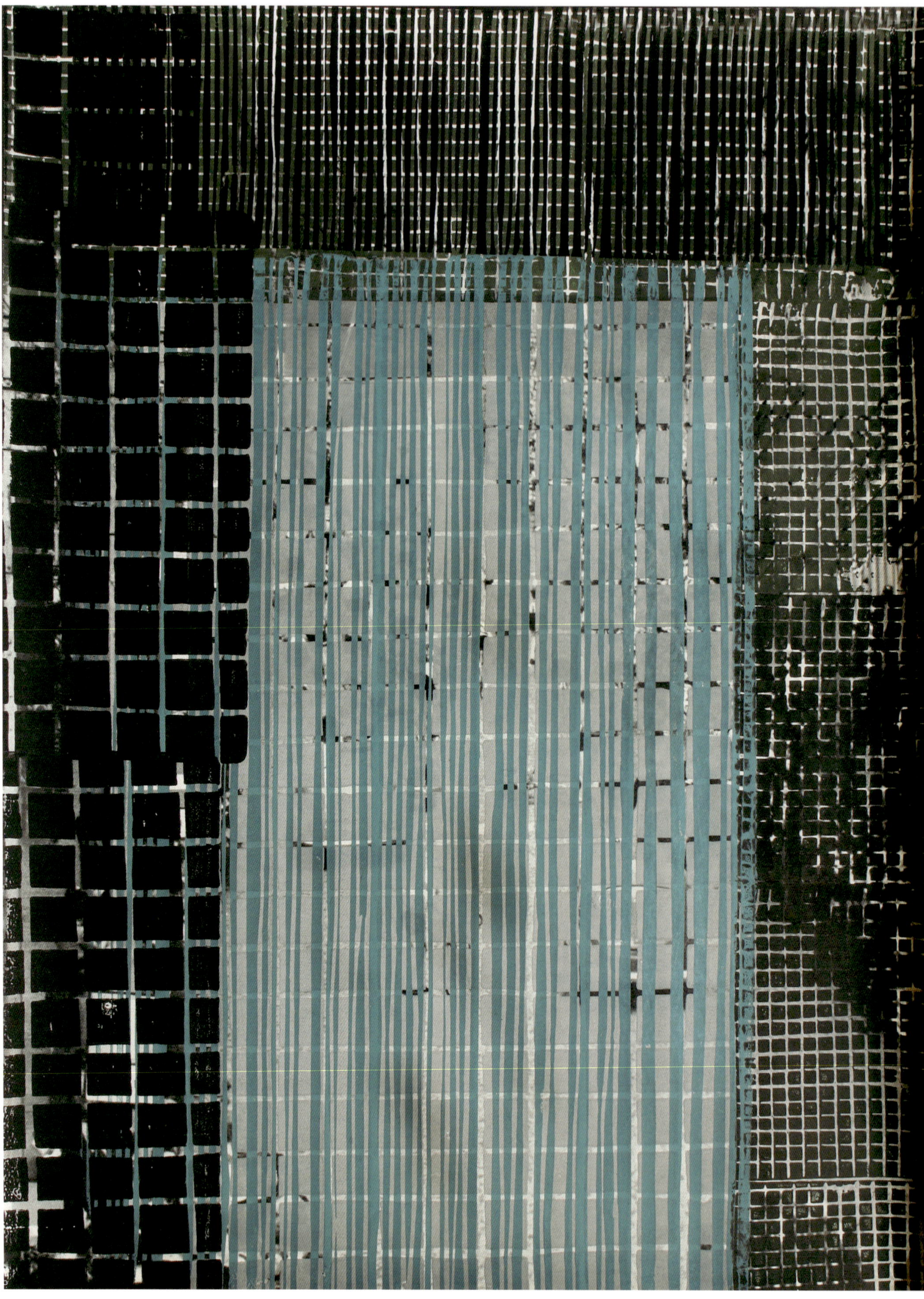

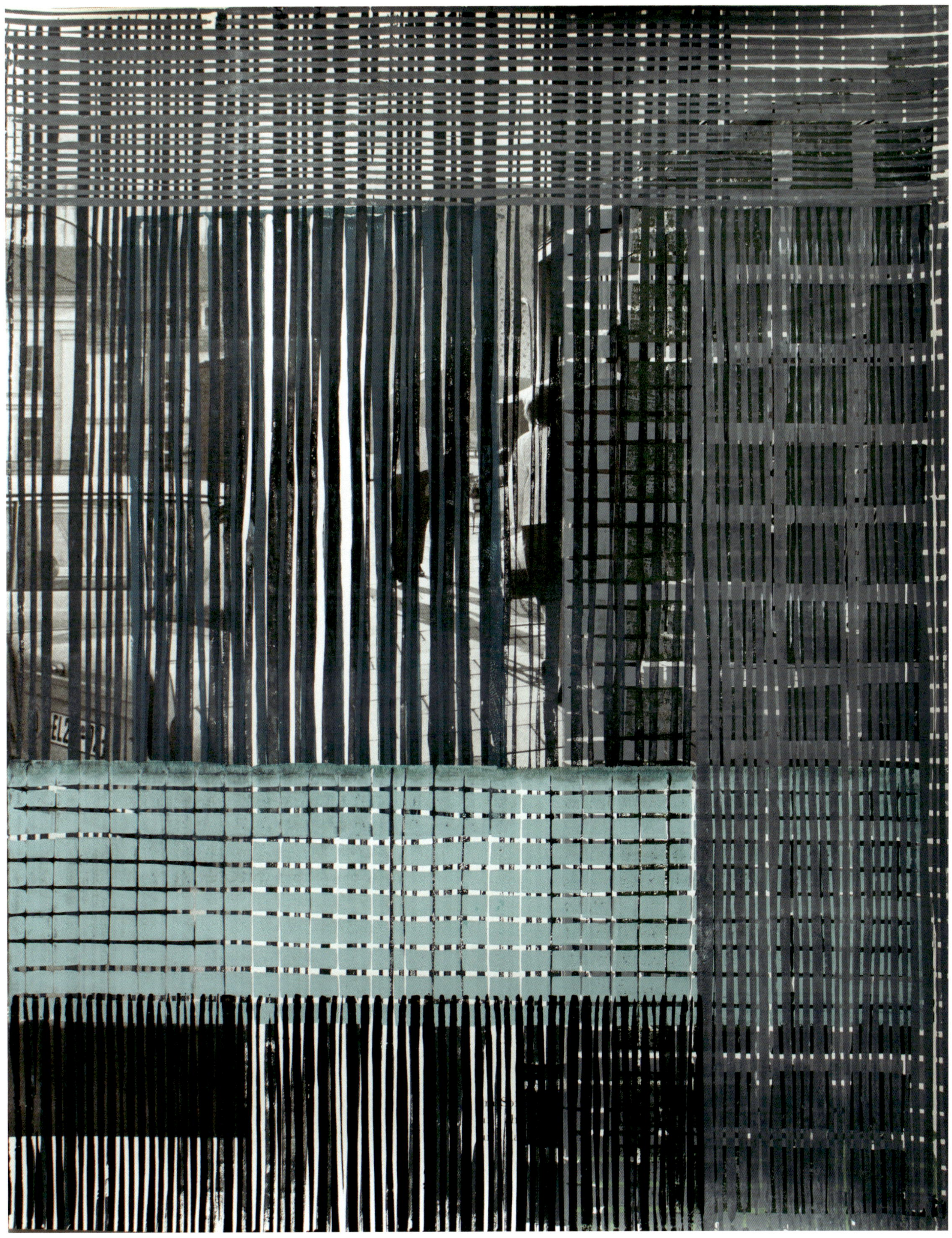

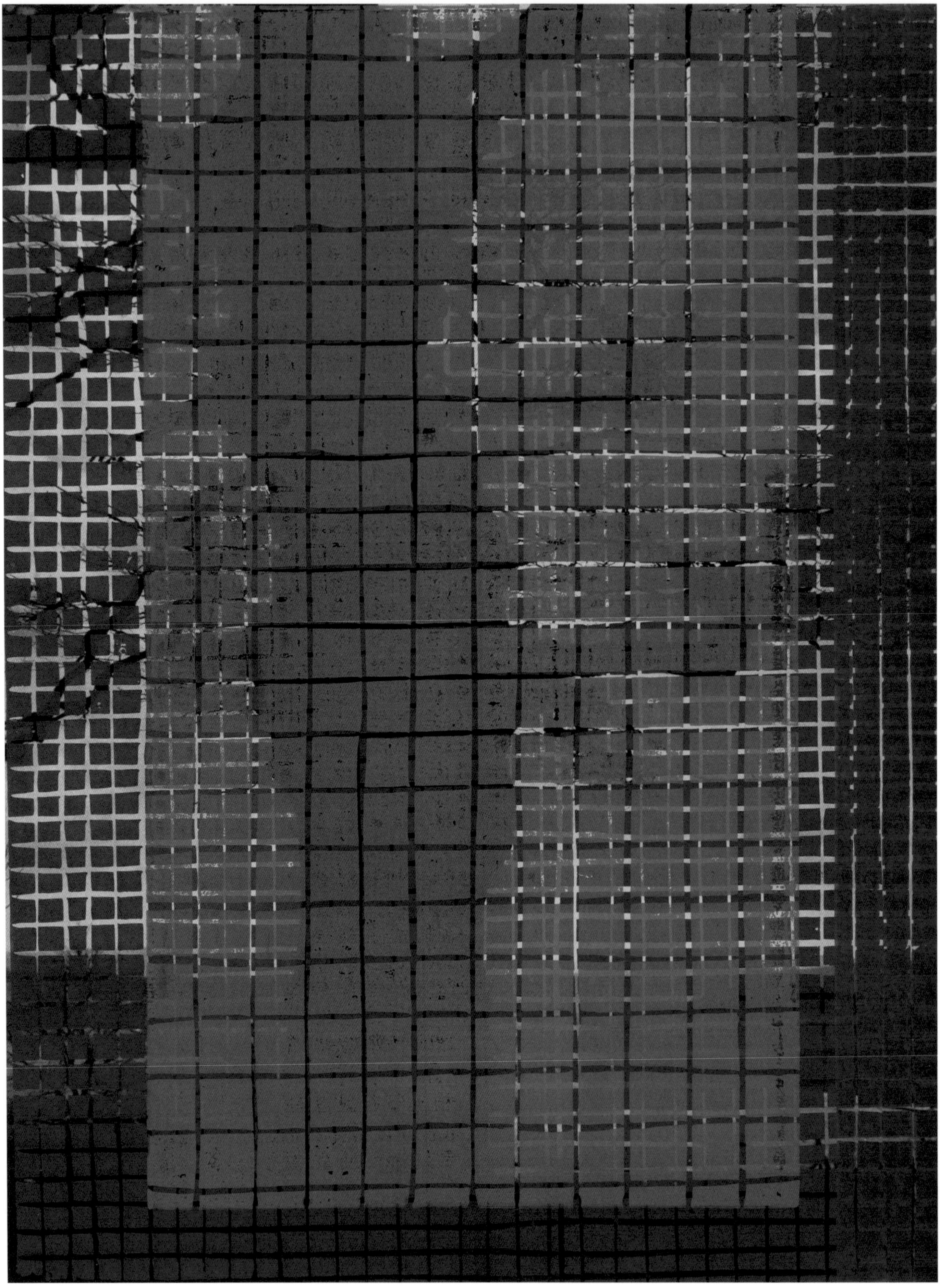

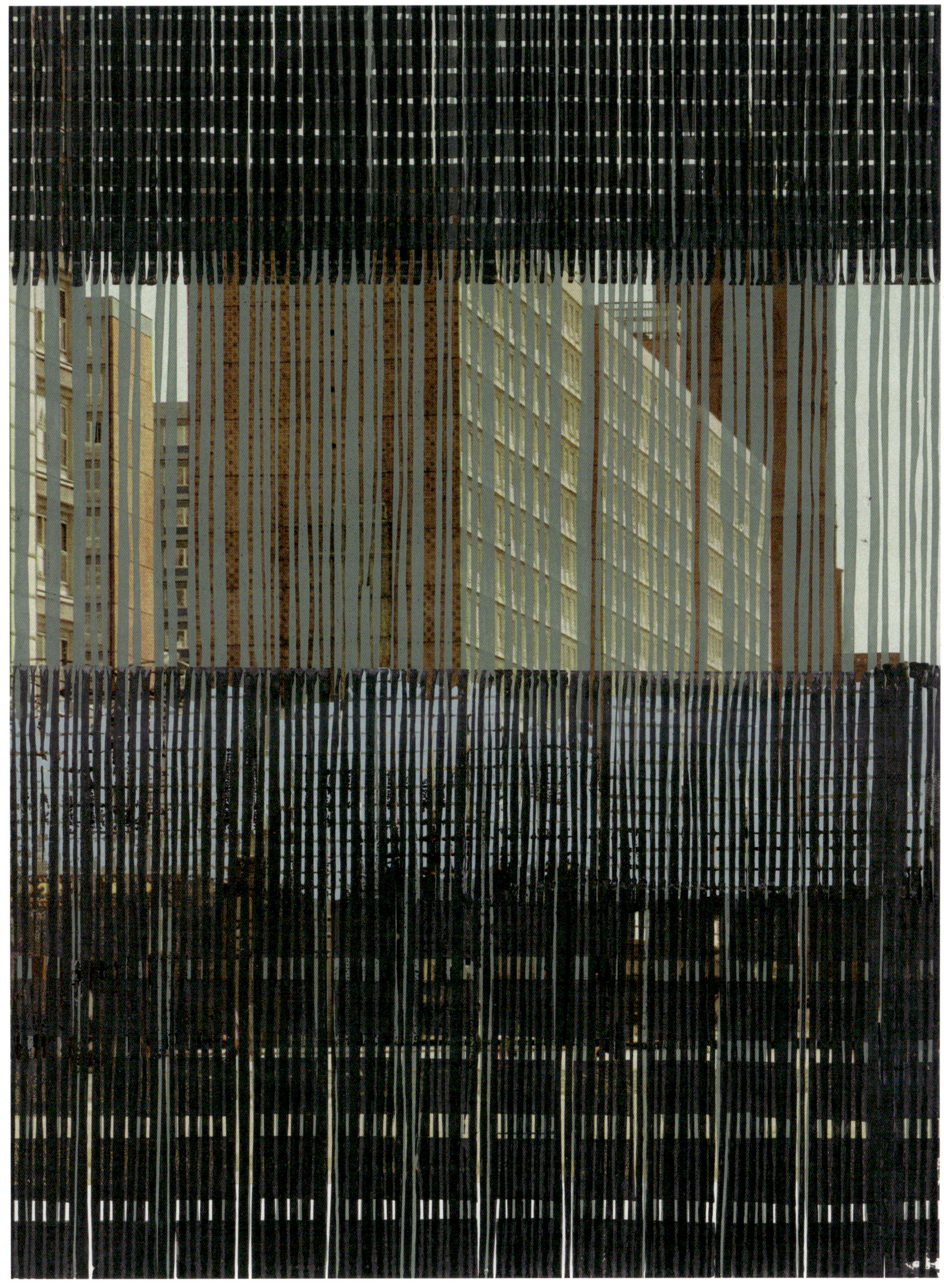

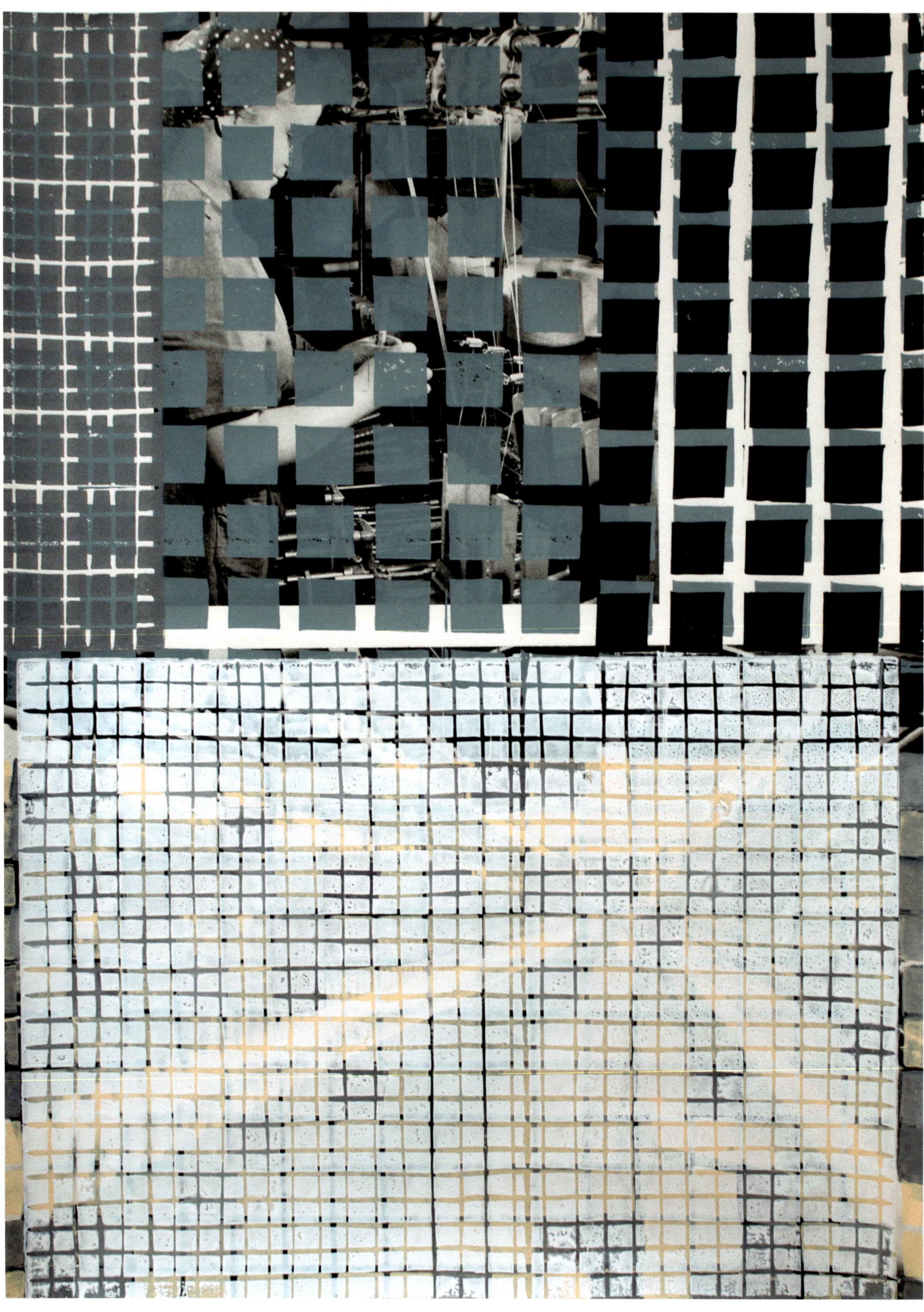

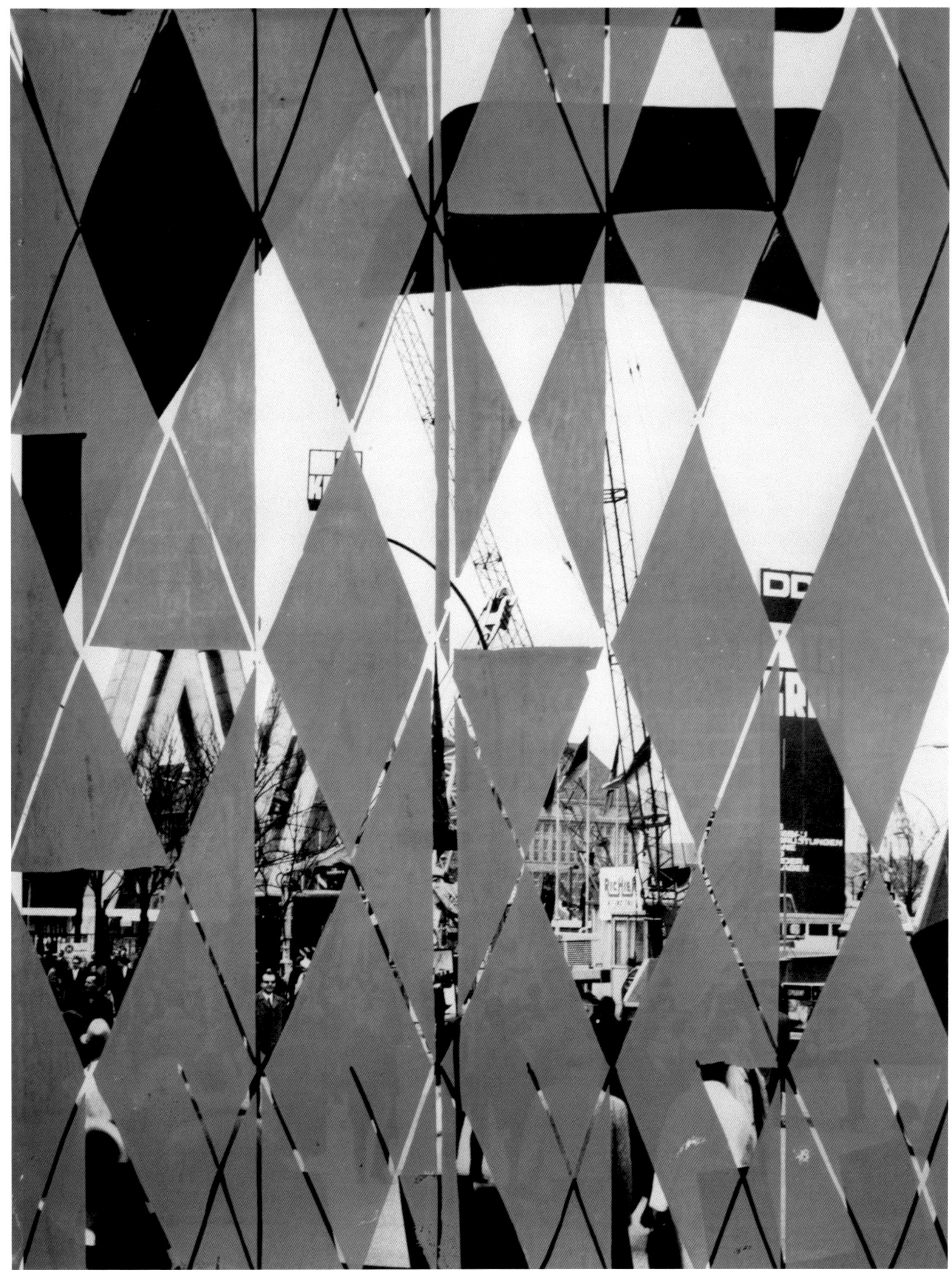

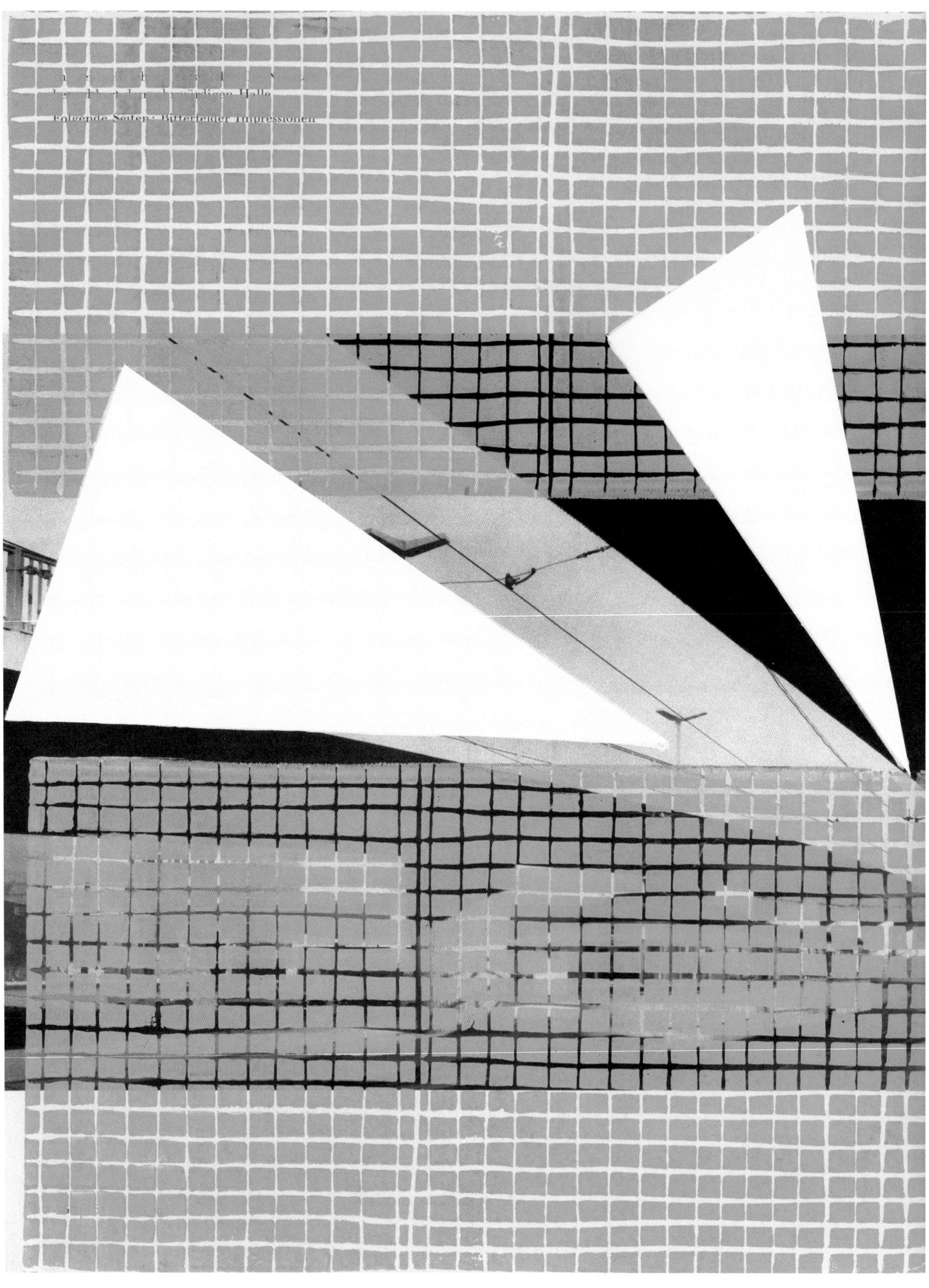
Folgende Seiten: Bitterfelder Impressionen

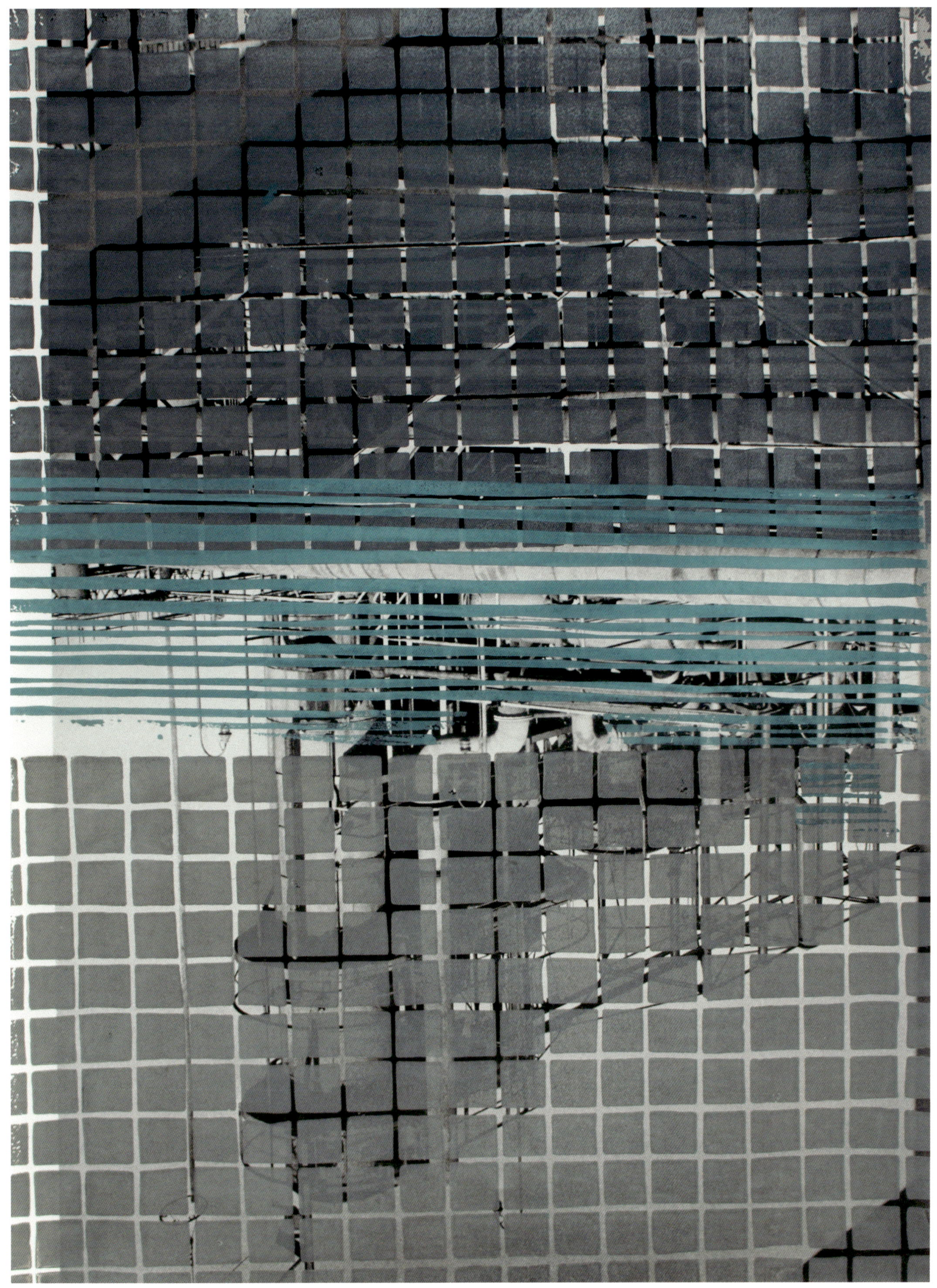

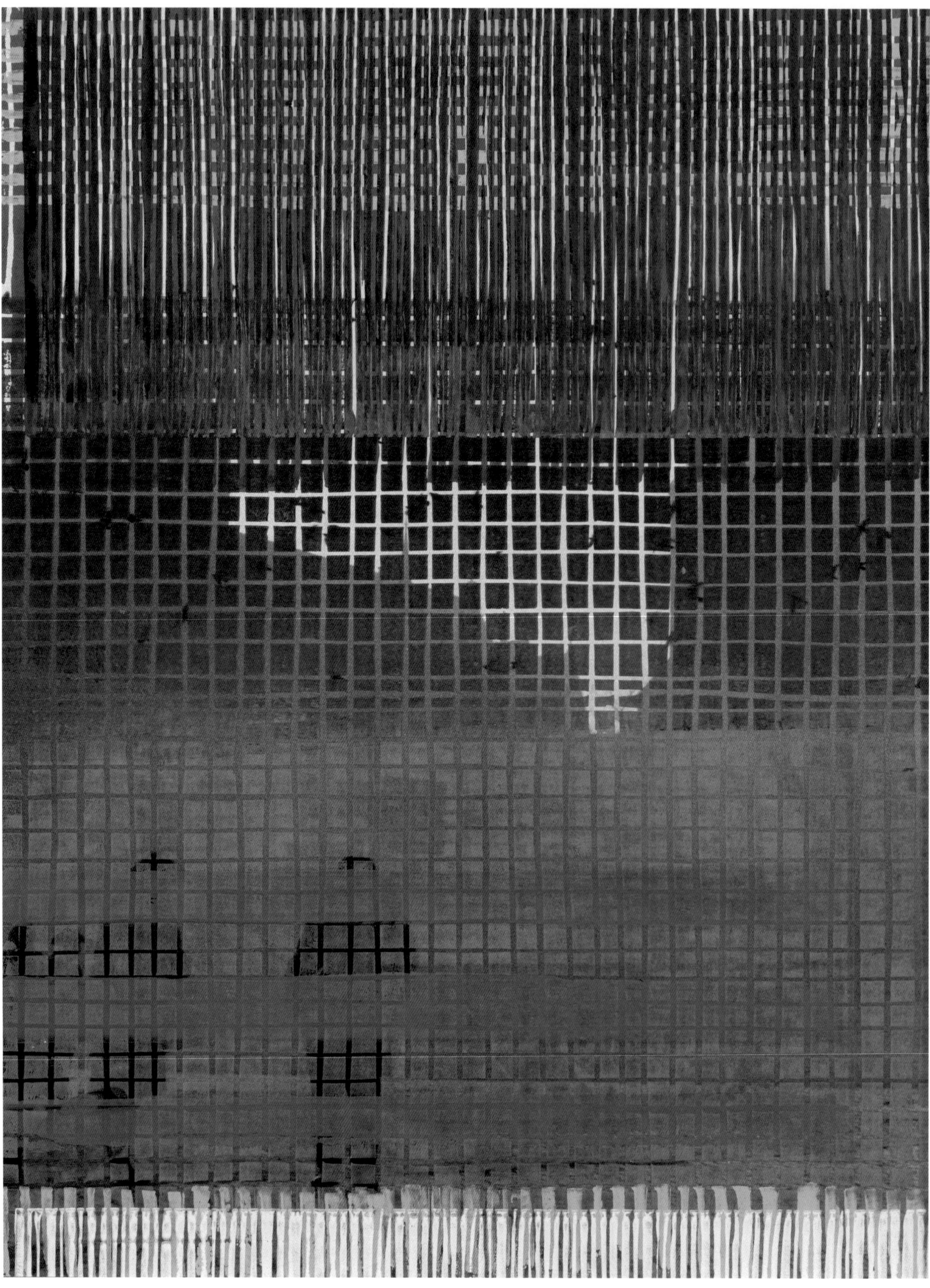

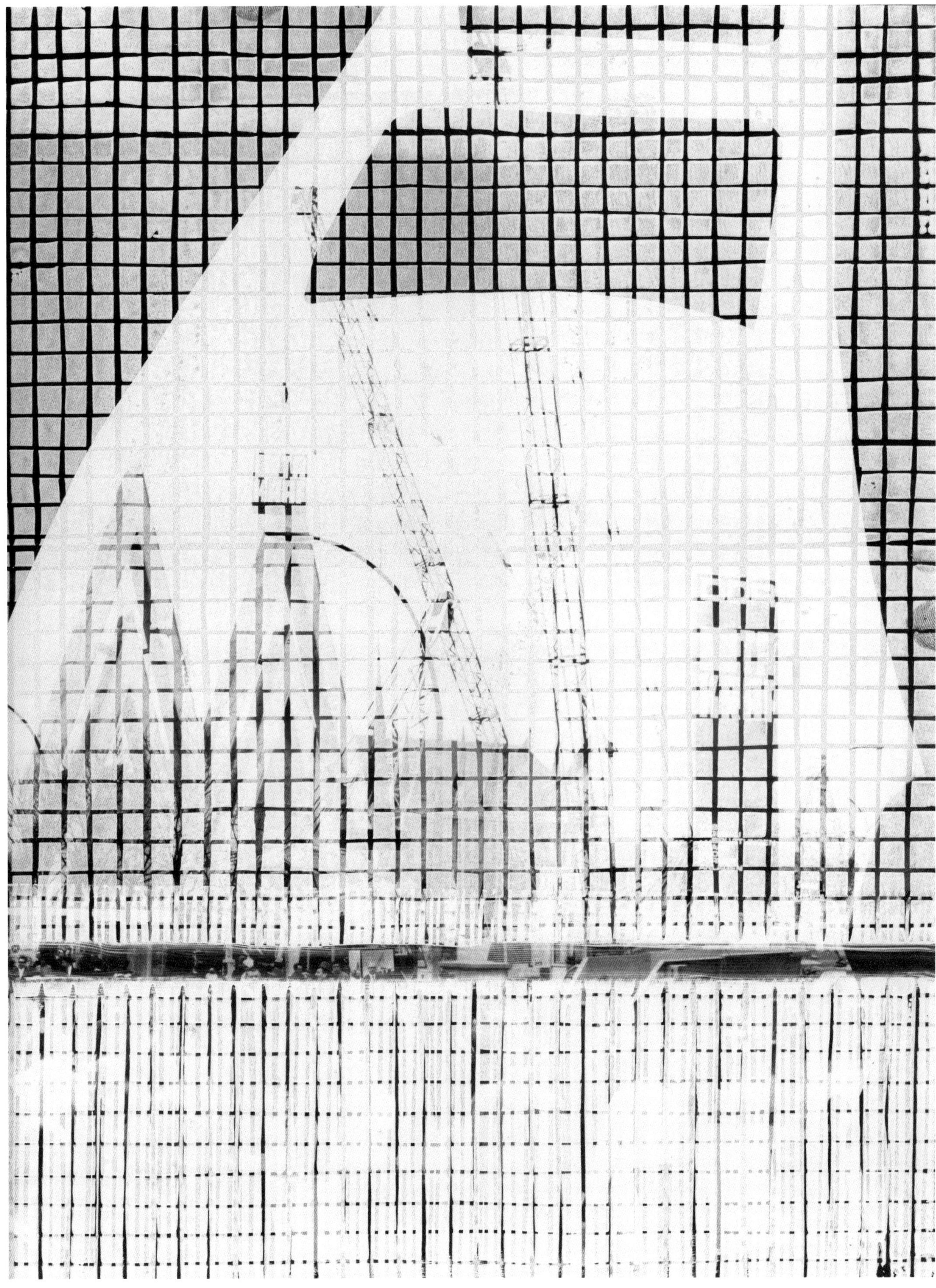

SCRAPING AND LAYERING THE PRESENT

BIRGIT EFFINGER

In our current situation of rampant events, the plethora of cultural and media interfaces gives rise to a scattered overall impression in which our gaze becomes blurred. In urban space, the visual messages of cultural and consumer goods flit by us en passant: they stray along our paths, circulate in the symbolic and economic order, sometimes taxing our perception, transport cultural myths as well as convictions, and evoke memories. The latter are particularly activated when our perception encounters vivid moments and elements we relate to personally, where concrete experiences come into play that are linked with pleasant and unpleasant mental images and connect the present with the past.

Katja Pudor is interested in this complex temporal situation: she inquires into the relationships between the present and recent past, between presence and absence. Her interest is chiefly directed at processes of transformation, at the shift in historical positings of meaning, as well as the superimposition of various temporal planes. She understands, for example, built architecture beyond its functionally planned forms of use as a legible, as it were archaeological field. For Pudor, walking in the city is a format for focusing our perception of historically shaped urban landscapes and to recognize urban processes and dynamics. To her mind, this makes it possible to actively experience the confusion and adjacency of various times and architectural configurations: each walk leads along streets and buildings from various eras and confronts us with the architecture, events, and contradictions of periods past. While Katja Pudor's artistic practice does not necessarily follow chronological developments or urban dramaturgies, it is shaped by affective entanglements and superimpositions of the real and the imagined. She thus works with photographs whose motifs have been familiar to her since her childhood, which she then, to her surprise and astonishment, rediscovered in illustrated volumes during her explorations of the city.

Abb. 1
Protocols of Remembering #19, 2019, linocut from multiple plates on book page, 29,7 × 22,7 cm

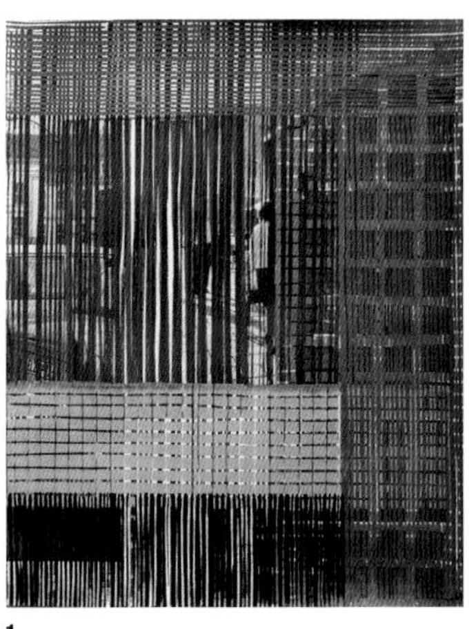
1

The starting point for the series *Protocols of Remembering* (2019) are two coffee-table books that she found, both published during the years before 1989: *Berlin: Hauptstadt der DDR A–Z* (Berlin: Capital of the GDR A–Z), published between 1959 and 1985, and the book *DDR: Deutsche Demokratische Republik* (GDR: German Democratic Republic). Both were published in several printings by F. A. Brockhaus Verlag in Leipzig until the late 1980s. The illustrations in the volumes show prominent buildings in Berlin and representative photographs of the cities of the GDR that were taken after the war, when the entire republic had completed its first phase of planned reconstruction. For the editors of the illustrated volumes, it was clearly necessary to present the post-war transformation of the cities to document social and public progress. The two volumes convey the motto required of every work of literature, music, visual arts, and architecture: "national in form, socialist in content." For this reason, they were presented as gifts from the highest echelons of the party and government of the GDR and at diplomatic meetings. During the years of the GDR, the political propaganda photographs of GDR modernism circulated as a symbol for progress and participation in the media, in the architectural history of the GDR, and in everyone's minds. After reunification, these visualized utopias of East German modernism were immediately discarded and landed in used bookstores, in the trash, or on the street.

Katja Pudor's relationship to these supposedly outdated visual narratives is pensive rather than cynical. Approaching the language of these images means expanding one's own customary view of the framework of architectural and urban illustrations in favor of new constellations, defining the situation in which the photographs are encountered, bringing one's own ideas and memories up to date, and giving the images a new time and structure. Removing individual photographs from the ideological context that once gave the images their meaning leads in several steps to stratifications, superimpositions, and re-formations. Overprinting in several layers reduces the recognition effect of the architectural structures significantly; the motifs become abstract, ambivalent, puzzling. The repetitive printed pattern covers over recognizable details and lends the images new visual rhythms; the aesthetic appropriation and overlapping of the visual narratives give rise to new aesthetic experiences.

GEGENWART SCHÜRFEN UND SCHICHTEN

In unserem derzeitigen Szenario der wuchernden Ereignisse verdichtet sich die Fülle der Kultur- und Medienoberflächen zu einem diffusen Gesamteindruck, in dem der Blick schwimmt. Im Stadtraum streifen uns en passant die visuellen Botschaften von Kultur- und Konsumgütern; sie streunen auf unseren Wegen, zirkulieren in der symbolischen und ökonomischen Ordnung, strapazieren zuweilen unsere Wahrnehmung, transportieren kulturelle Mythen wie auch Überzeugungen und evozieren Erinnerungen. Letztere werden besonders dort aktiviert, wo unsere Wahrnehmung auf bedeutsame Momente und persönliche Bezüge stößt, wo konkrete Erfahrungen mit im Spiel sind, die mit angenehmen wie unangenehmen Vorstellungsbildern verknüpft werden und die Gegenwart mit der Vergangenheit verzahnen.

Katja Pudor interessiert sich für diese zeitliche Gemengelage; sie befragt die Beziehungen zwischen Gegenwart und jüngster Vergangenheit, zwischen Präsenz und Absenz. Ihr Interesse gilt vor allem Prozessen der Transformation, der Verschiebung von historischen Bedeutungssetzungen wie auch der Überlagerung von verschiedenen temporären Ebenen. So begreift sie beispielsweise gebaute Architektur jenseits ihrer funktional geplanten Gebrauchsformen als lesbares, gleichsam archäologisches Feld. Das Gehen in der Stadt ist für Pudor ein Format, um die Wahrnehmung für historisch geformte Stadtlandschaften zu schärfen und urbane Prozesse und Dynamiken zu erkennen. Für sie macht es das Durcheinander und Nebeneinander von unterschiedlichen Zeiten und architektonischen Konfigurationen erfahrbar; jeder Gang führt an Straßenzügen und Bauwerken aus

It is thus virtually impossible for viewers to think of the images in terms of what they originally depicted. Instead, printed over and distorted, the images are more like a palimpsest, a "mystic writing pad" that preserves all printed traces, superimposing them and allowing them to appear in layered form. The technique of the palimpsest, a surface that is reinscribed over and over again, was used in antiquity and the Middle Ages for cost reasons due to the scarcity of material, since papyrus and later parchment were very expensive and difficult to manufacture. Since the nineteenth century, the palimpsest advanced several times to become a conceptual figure for the creative process and a metaphor for the mechanisms of memory. A prominent example of the metaphor of the palimpsest is Sigmund Freud's concept of the human apparatus of perception and memory: in his "Note upon the 'Mystic Writing Pad,'" published in 1925, he depicts the operation of memory as a continuous layering, superimposition, and reconfiguration of knowledge, perception, and experience. According to Freud, our brain is shaped by the constant addition of layers and offers unlimited capacity for absorption and for permanent memory traces, which of course lie hidden and are only accessible in exceptional cases. The structure of the palimpsest, layered several times over, proves, like our brain, to be both storage and the object of permanent reformatting. In the sense of the metaphor of the palimpsest, overwriting does not mean deleting. Indeed, characteristic for the palimpsest is that everything new builds up on what preceded it, the entire past exists in the present, and the individual layers enter into a dialogical relationship with one another.

Accordingly, Katja Pudor's compressions in the printing process are always already acts of creating a palimpsest, in which not only images and texts, but also processes of memory and layers of meaning overwrite one another and are reconfigured. Each newly added layer references something pre-existing and reshapes the given with the printed matrix. This matrix allows previous visual decisions to be multiplied, revising or modifying the emergent image. With the help of the print matrix, advance within the process can also be documented as a path taken and can thus be followed, in a literal sense, as a log. The technique of placing layers on top of one another, of allowing an ever-greater complexity to emerge, can also be found in the series *Urania Universum* (2018). For this body of work, the artist chose several pages from two volumes of the book series of the same name. The popular science series contains thirty-six volumes of yearbooks for science, technology, culture, sport, and entertainment and was published by Urania Verlag in Leipzig and Jena from 1955 (vol. 1) to 1990 (vol. 36). Katja Pudor printed several pages of the 1968 yearbook succes-

---

unterschiedlichen Epochen entlang und konfrontiert uns mit Gebäuden, Ergebnissen und Widersprüchen vergangener Zeiten. Katja Pudors künstlerische Praxis folgt freilich nicht zwangsläufig chronologischen Entwicklungen oder stadtpolitischen Dramaturgien, sondern ist vielmehr geprägt durch affektive Verwicklungen und Überschneidungen von Wirklichem und Imaginiertem. So arbeitet sie mit Fotografien, deren Motive ihr seit der Kindheit vertraut sind, die sie dann auf ihren Streifzügen durch die Stadt in Bildbänden wiederentdeckt hat und überrascht und verwundert war.

Ausgangspunkt für die Serie *Protocols of remembering* (2019) sind zwei gefundene, opulente Bildbände, die in der Vorwendezeit veröffentlicht wurden. Zum einen ist dies der zwischen 1959 und 1985 erschienene Band *Berlin – Hauptstadt der DDR von A–Z*, zum anderen handelt es sich um das Buch *DDR – Deutsche Demokratische Republik*. Beide Publikationen wurden in mehreren Auflagen bis Ende der achtziger Jahre vom F. A. Brockhaus Verlag Leipzig veröffentlicht. Die Abbildungen in den Bänden zeigen prominente Gebäude in Berlin wie auch repräsentative Städtebilder der DDR, die nach dem Krieg fotografiert wurden, als die gesamte demokratische Republik die erste Phase des planmäßigen Wiederaufbaus bereits hinter sich hatte. Für die Herausgeber der Bildbände lag es offensichtlich auf der Hand, den Wandel der Städte nach dem Krieg abzubilden, um damit auch den gesellschaftlichen und öffentlichen Fortschritt zu dokumentieren. Beide Bände tranportieren die Losung, die an sämtliche Werke der Literatur, der Musik, der bildenden Kunst und auch an die Architektur herangetragen wurde: national in der Form, sozialistisch im Inhalt. Aus diesem Grund wurden die Bände von höchsten Stellen aus Partei und Regierung der DDR auch bei diplomatischen Treffen verschenkt. Zu DDR-Zeiten kursierten die politisch-propagandistisch motivierten Fotografien

Abb. 2
Manipulating the Archive, 2019, performance, duration: 30 min
Different media on different papers, Kunstquartier Bethanien / Studio 1, Berlin, installation and performance as a part of the group show *the horizon looks different from afar/* pilote contemporary

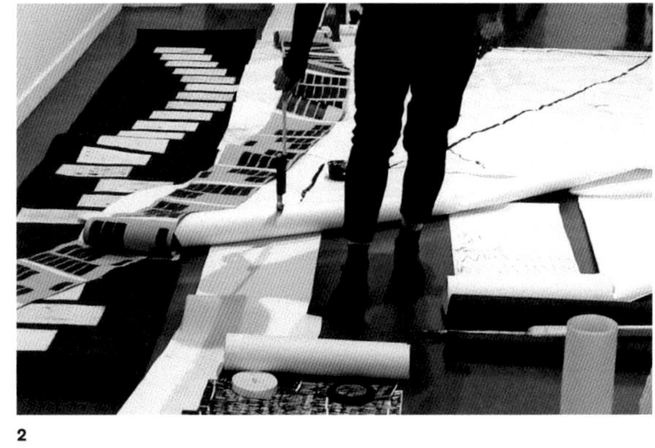
2

sively with printing plates created especially for this purpose. With each successive printing, less of the original information is visible. While the individual layers of print cannot be entirely controlled in the framework of the printing process, they do not come about entirely accidentally or independently of one another, and they make the original text almost completely disappear. Thus, the repeated overprinting of the pronounced certainties in *Urania Universum* with patterns and grids takes the original text to a realm that encompasses processes of both memory and imagination. The reason for this is that the title of the series ensures that the hidden subtext – even if beneath the surface and concealed from our gaze – remains constantly present. As in the palimpsest or the "mystic writing pad," the original text is both present and absent at the same time. The minute remaining particles and traces of text that shimmer through the printed visual elements evoke various structures and conceptions of time: linear, running parallel to one another, or as a permanent present. Every printed layer of *Urania Universum* develops its own visual options, for vinyl printing offers the possibility of creating various intermediate prints with compositions and pictorial constellations all their own. In this way, the artist's visual motifs take us on a journey whose point of departure is conceptually fixed but whose outcome remains open. Thinking and artistic practice subject themselves as a kind of thought practice to the creative process, whose figures of perception and compositional arrangements are as unpredictable as the course of Pudor's performances. *Manipulating the Archive* (2018–2019) was presented by Katja Pudor at various locations in performances lasting from thirty to forty minutes. With the performance, the artist enters into a selfdefined playing field of experimentation. In slow, flowing movements, she arranges largescale banners of paper according to their texture and quality—folded, unfolded, written, unwritten. The banners and piles of paper change their form and shape from performance to performance and thus jut into the present situation as the remains of earlier performances. There are also drawings, print arrangements, and other materials from the artistic archive. The artist uses these circumstances to

---

der DDR-Moderne als Symbol für Fortschritt und Teilhabe in den Medien, in der Architekturgeschichte der DDR und in jedermanns Köpfen. In der Nachwendezeit wurden die bildgewordenen Utopien der Ost-Moderne im Handumdrehen ausgemustert und landeten in Antiquariaten, im Papiermüll oder auf der Straße.

Katja Pudor hat zu diesen vermeintlich überholten Bildnarrativen kein zynisches, sondern ein nachdenkliches Verhältnis. Mit der Sprache dieser Bilder umgehen heißt: Den eigenen, gewohnten Blick auf die Gefüge der Architektur- und Städteabbildungen zugunsten neuer Konstellationen zu öffnen, die Situation der Begegnung mit den Fotografien zu bestimmen, die eigenen Vorstellungen und Erinnerungen zu aktualisieren und den Bildern eine neue Zeit und eine neue Struktur zu geben. Das Herausnehmen einzelner Fotografien aus dem ideologischen Kontext, der den Bildern einstmals Bedeutung verliehen hat, führt in weiteren Schritten zu Schichtungen, Überlagerungen und Umbildungen. Das Überdrucken in mehreren Schichten mindert den Wiedererkennungseffekt der baulichen Gefüge erheblich, die Motive werden abstrakt, vieldeutig, rätselhaft. Der gedruckte, musterartige Rapport überblendet erkennbare Details und verleiht den Bildern neue Bildrhythmen, die ästhetische Aneignung und Überlagerung der Bildnarrative eröffnen neue ästhetische Erfahrungen. Daher ist es für die Betrachter*innen schier unmöglich, die Bilder vom ursprünglich Abgebildeten her zu denken. Die überdruckten und überformten Bilder gleichen vielmehr einem Palimpsest – einem „Wunderblock" – der alle Druckspuren aufbewahrt, überlagert und in einer Schichtungsform erscheinen lässt. Die Technik des Palimpsestierens – des Wiederbeschreibens – wurde in der Antike und im Mittelalter noch aus Kostengründen und aufgrund von Materialknappheit angewendet, da Papyrus und später Pergament sehr teuer und aufwendig

bring herself into play on site: the situational mood, the physical space, time, the spreading and overlapping of papers, the targeted brush strokes over the piles of paper, the new compositions emerging and the artists' bodies are all equal playing figures in the artistic process. The stage-like setting allows spectators to take part in the various movement dynamics in space and the assemblage-like consideration of possibilities and layers, in minute alterations. Thus, in fluid sequences of motion, the artist marks with broad brushstrokes the upper layers of the piles of paper, which after some time are made to disappear. Every moment of the artistic action, each minimal revision heightens attention to the overall situation. Each thing, each moment becomes significant and, like the discarded moments of East German modernism, is filled with new life.

Katja Pudor's artistic practice thus initiates a kind of metamorphosis in which once significant things, existing ascriptions of meaning, or specific constellations take on a different shape and thus expand the receptive interface of our present. In the process, Pudor's apparently retrospective re-inscriptions and reformattings prove to be fine, delicate seismographs of a present in the process of emerging. ■

---

in der Herstellung waren. Seit dem 19. Jahrhundert avancierte das Palimpsest dann mehrfach zur Denkfigur für kreative Prozesse wie auch zur Metapher für Erinnerungsvorgänge. Prominentes Beispiel einer Palimpsest-Metaphorik ist Sigmund Freuds Konzept des menschlichen Wahrnehmungs- und Gedächtnisapparats: In seiner 1925 veröffentlichten Notiz über den „Wunderblock" entwirft er die Gedächtnisleistung als kontinuierliche Schichtung, Überlagerung und Neukonfiguration von Wissen, Wahrnehmungen und Erfahrungen. Unser Gehirn wird laut Freud also durch permanenten Schichtenzuwachs geformt und bietet unbegrenzte Aufnahmefähigkeiten wie ebenso dauerhafte Erinnerungsspuren, die freilich im Verborgenen liegen und nur in Ausnahmefällen verfügbar sind. Die mehrfach geschichtete Struktur des Palimpsests erweist sich wie unser Gehirn als Speicher und zugleich als Objekt permanenter Neuformatierung. Überschreiben bedeutet im Sinne der Palimpsest-Metaphorik keineswegs Löschen. Kennzeichnend für das Palimpsest ist vielmehr, dass jedes Neue auf Vorangegangenem aufbaut, jedes Vergangene im Gegenwärtigen existiert, und die einzelnen Schichten miteinander in eine dialogische Beziehung treten.

Dementsprechend sind Katja Pudors Verdichtungen im druckgrafischen Prozess immer auch Akte des Palimpsestierens, bei denen nicht nur Bilder und Texte, sondern auch Erinnerungsprozesse und Sinnebenen überschrieben und rekonfiguriert werden. Jede neu hinzukommende Schicht nimmt auf Vorhandenes Bezug und überformt mit der druckgrafischen Matrix das Gegebene. Diese Matrix erlaubt es, einmal getroffene gestalterische Entscheidungen zu vervielfältigen, das entstehende Bild zu revidieren oder zu modifizieren. Mithilfe der Druckmatrix kann das prozessuale Voranschreiten auch als zurückgelegter Weg dokumentiert und damit als Protokoll im wortwörtlichen Sinne nachvollziehbar werden. Das Verfahren der übereinander gelegten Schichten, die eine immer höhere Komplexität entstehen lassen, findet sich auch in der Serie *Urania Universum* (2018). Die Künstlerin wählt für diesen Werkzyklus einzelne Blätter aus zwei Bänden der gleichnamigen Buchreihe aus. Die populärwissenschaftliche Buchreihe umfasst 36 Bände von Jahrbüchern für Wissenschaft, Technik, Kultur, Sport und Unterhaltung und wurde vom Urania Verlag in Leipzig und Jena zwischen 1955 (Band 1) und 1990 (Band 36) herausgegeben. Katja Pudor hat einzelne Seiten des Jahrbuchs von 1968 sukzessiv mit eigens dafür hergestellten Druckplatten bedruckt. Mit jedem Druckvorgang ist weniger von den ursprünglichen Informationen sichtbar. Die einzelnen Druckschichten lassen sich im Rahmen des Druckprozesses zwar nicht vollständig kontrollieren, sie entstehen jedoch nicht zufällig und unabhängig voneinander und bringen den Ausgangstext fast vollständig zum Verschwinden. Der mannigfache Überdruck der verlautbarten Gewissheiten im *Urania Universum* mit Mustern und Rastern überführt den ursprünglichen Text sonach in einen Bereich, der einerseits Prozesse des Erinnerns, aber auch jene der Imagination umfasst. Denn der Titel der Serie hält uns den verborgenen Subtext – wenngleich unter der Oberfläche und unseren Blicken entzogen – beständig präsent. Wie beim Palimpsest oder dem „Wunderblock" ist der Ursprungstext abwesend und anwesend zugleich. So rufen die winzigen Restpartikel und Textspuren, die zwischen den gedruckten Gestaltungselementen hervorblitzen, verschiedene Zeitstrukturen und -vorstellungen auf: linear, parallel ablaufend oder als permanente Gegenwart. Jeder Überdruck des *Urania Universum* entwickelt eigene Bildoptionen Denn der Vinyldruck bietet die Möglichkeit,

unterschiedliche Zustandsdrucke und jeweils eigene Kompositionen und Bildkonstellationen herzustellen. Auf diese Weise nehmen die Bildmotive die Künstlerin mit auf eine Reise, deren Ausgangspunkt zwar konzeptionell festgelegt, deren Ausgang dennoch offen ist. Denken und künstlerisches Handeln setzen sich in einer Art von denkerischem Handeln dem bildnerischen Prozess aus, dessen Wahrnehmungsfiguren und kompositorische Arrangements so wenig vorhersehbar sind wie der Verlauf von Pudors Performances. *Manipulating the Archive* (2018 – 2019) wurde von Katja Pudor an unterschiedlichen Orten mit unterschiedlicher Dauer zwischen 30 und 40 Minuten aufgeführt. Mit der Performance begibt sich die Künstlerin in ein selbst abgestecktes Spielfeld der Versuchsanordnung: Sie ordnet in langsamen, fließenden Bewegungen überdimensionale Papierbahnen entsprechend ihrer Beschaffenheit – gefaltet, ungefaltet, beschrieben, unbeschrieben – im Raum an. Diese Papierbahnen und Papierstapel ändern von Performance zu Performance ihre Form und Gestalt und ragen dann als Reste früherer Aufführungen in die gegenwärtige Situation hinein. Hinzu kommen Zeichnungen, Druckarrangements und weitere Materialien aus dem künstlerischen Archiv. Mit diesen Gegebenheiten bringt sich die Künstlerin vor Ort ins Spiel: Die situative Befindlichkeit, der physische Raum, die Zeit, das Ausbreiten und Überlagern der Papiere, die gezielte Pinselgeste über die Papierstapelungen, die entstehenden Neukompositionen wie auch der Künstlerinnenkörper sind gleichberechtigte Spielfiguren des künstlerischen Prozesses. Das bühnenartige Setting lässt die Zuschauer*innen an den unterschiedlichen Bewegungsdynamiken im Raum und an dem assemblageartigen Abwägen von Möglichkeiten, Schichten und an minutiösen Veränderungen teilhaben. So markiert die Künstlerin in fließenden Bewegungsabfolgen mit breiten Pinselstrichen die obereren Schichten von Papierstapeln, die nach geraumer Zeit dann wieder zum Verschwinden gebracht werden. Jeder Moment der künstlerischen Aktion, jede minimale Umgestaltung schärft die Aufmerksamkeit für die Gesamtsituation. So wird jedes Ding, jeder Moment des Handelns bedeutsam und füllt sich, wie die weggeworfenen Bücher der Ost-Moderne, mit neuem Leben. Katja Pudors künstlerische Praxis initiiert insofern eine Art Metamorphose, in der ehemals bedeutsame Dinge, vorhandene Sinnzuschreibungen oder spezifische Konstellationen eine andere Gestalt bekommen und so die Aufnahmeoberfläche unserer Gegenwart erweitern. Dabei erweisen sich Pudors scheinbar rückwärts orientierte Umschreibungen und Umformatierungen auch als feinnervige Seismografen einer Gegenwart, die erst im Entstehen ist. ▬

URANIA UNIVERSUM

Linocut from multiple
plates on book pages
2018

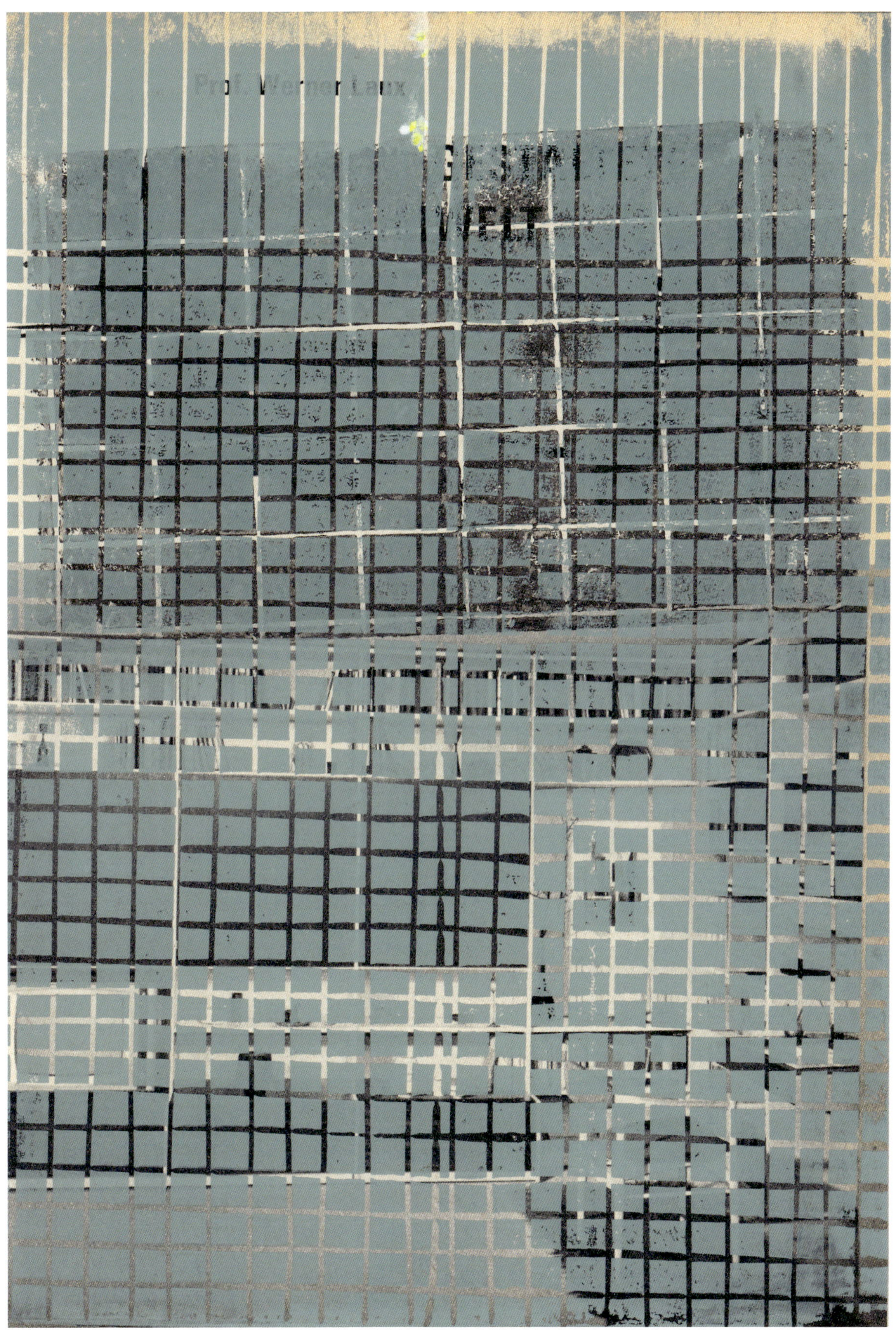
Prof. Werner Laux
WELT

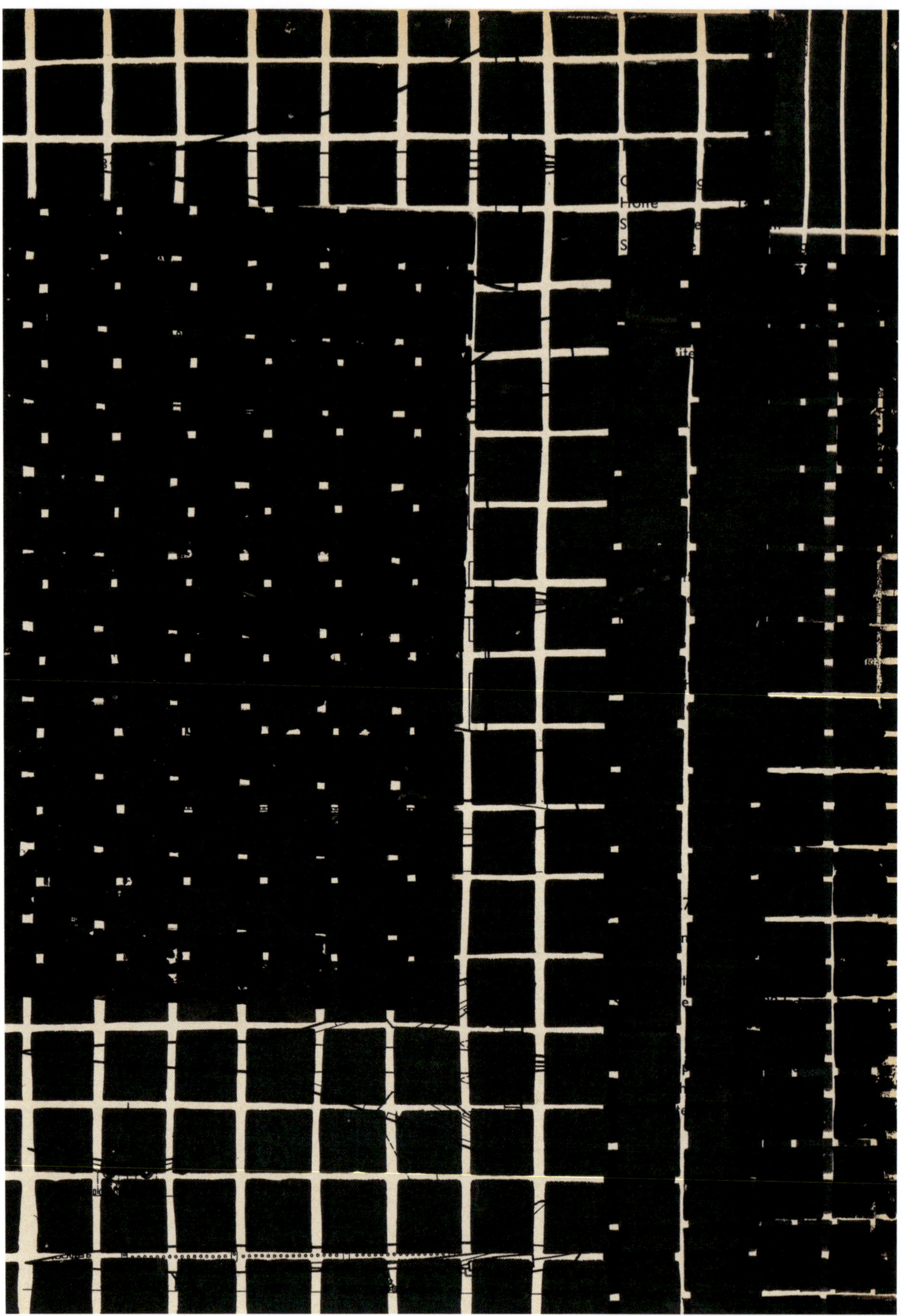

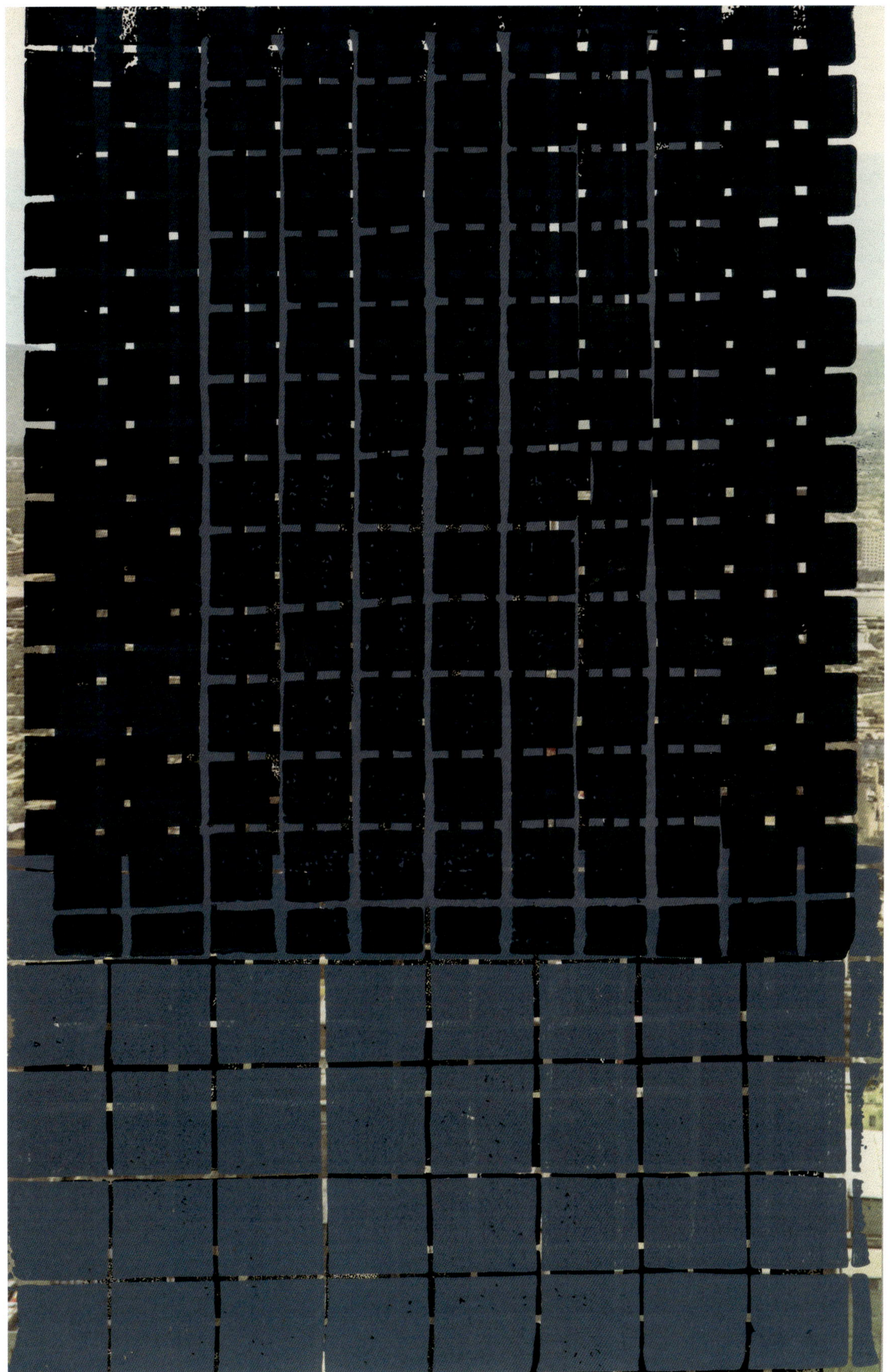

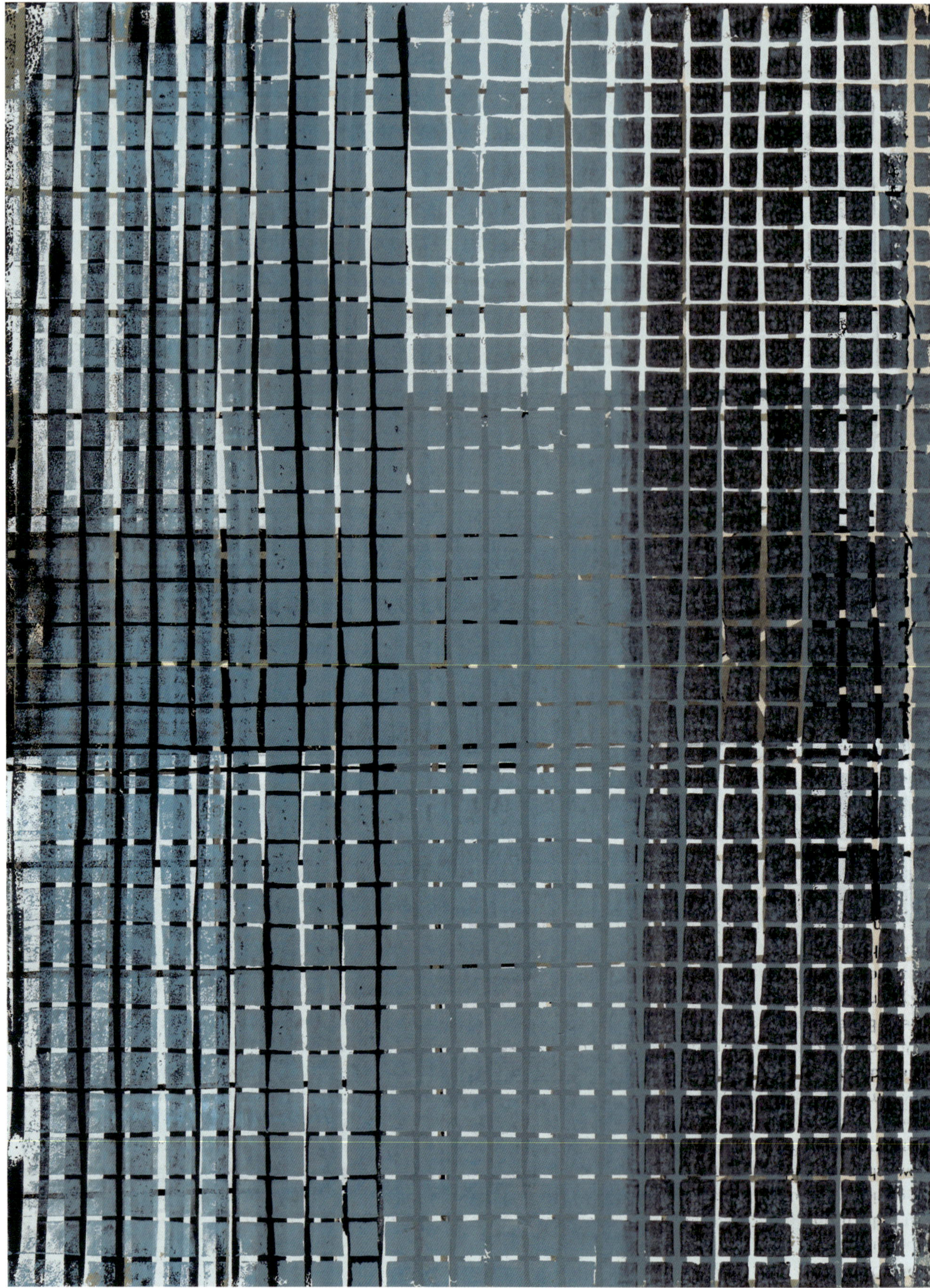

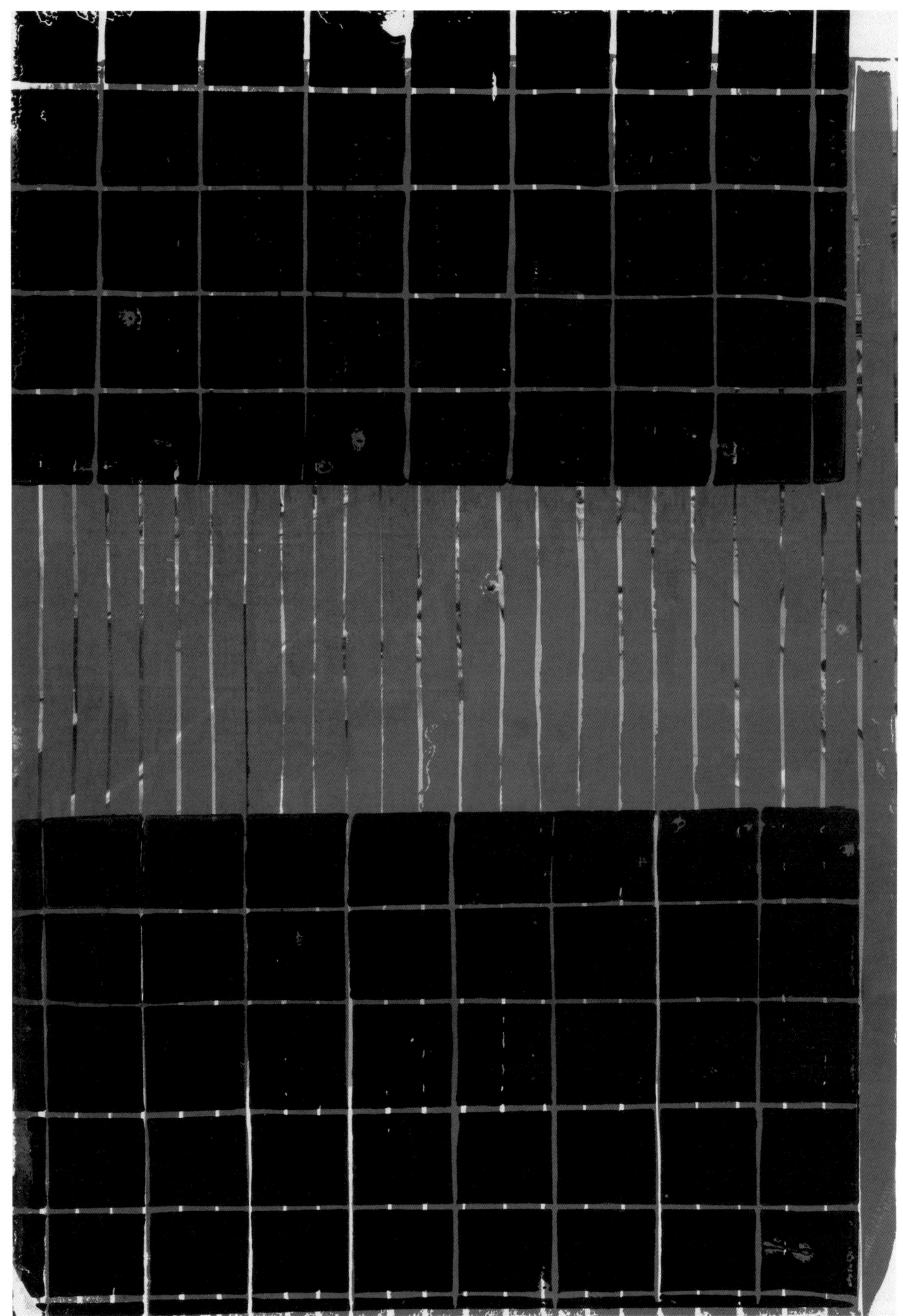

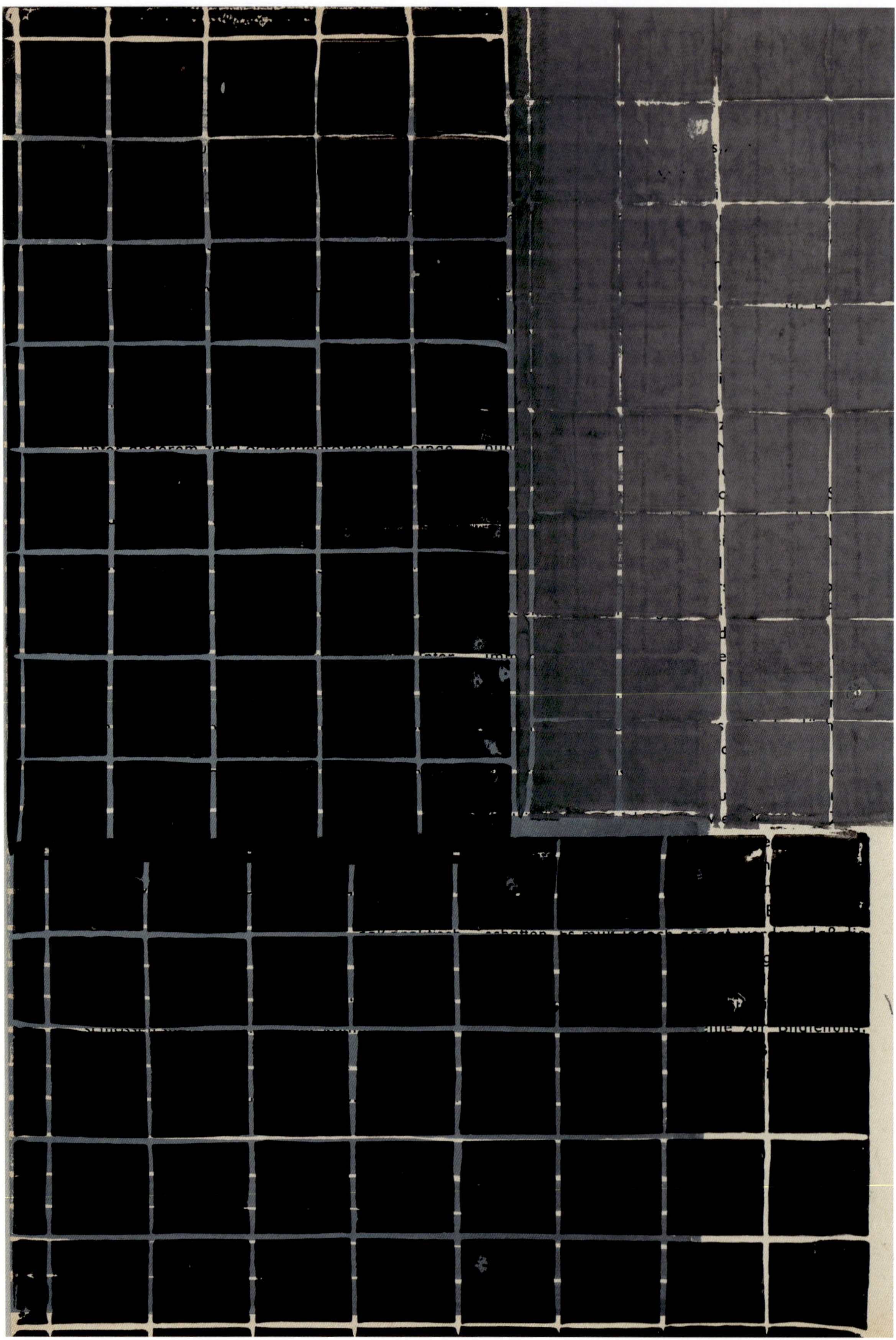

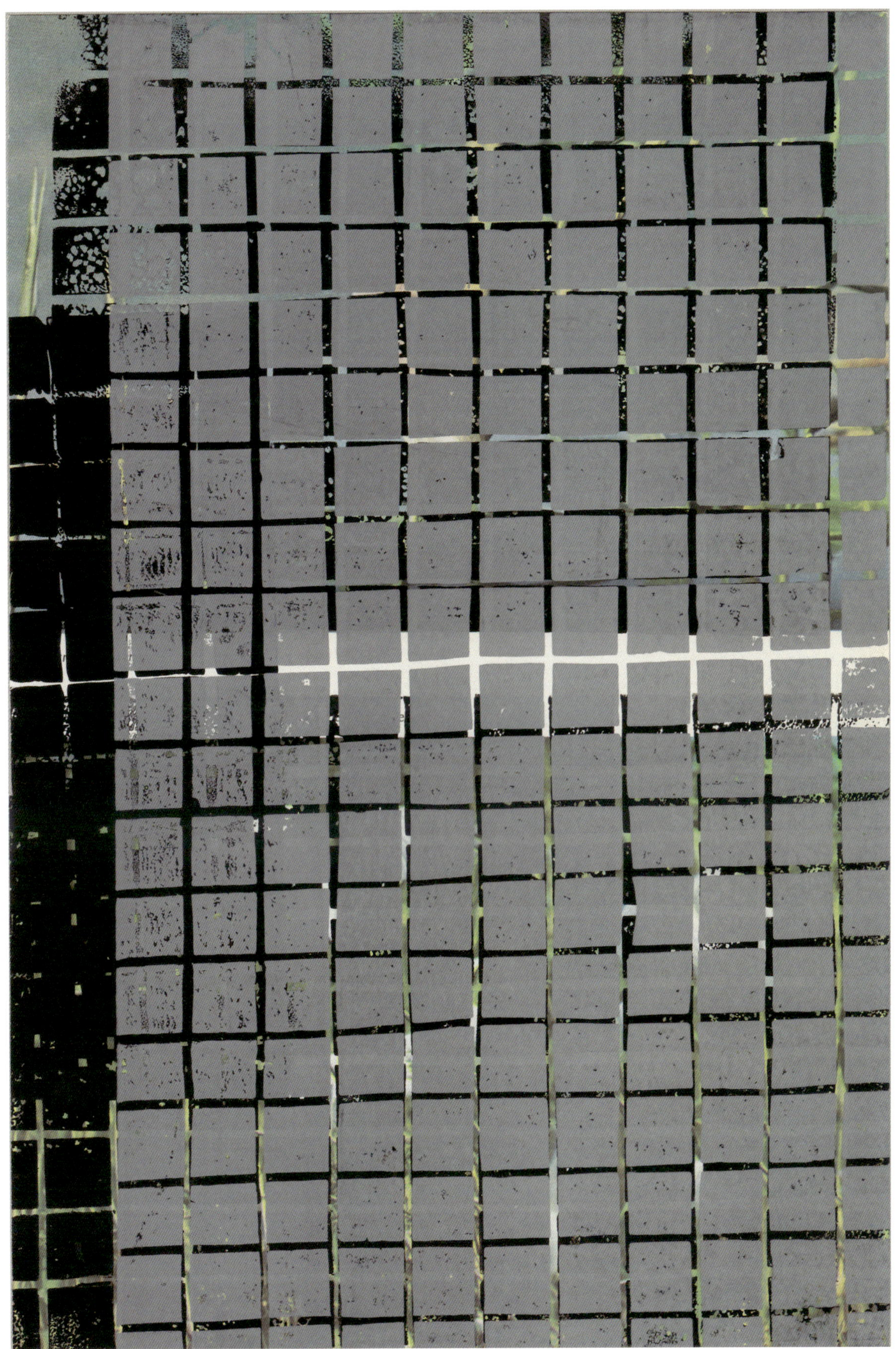

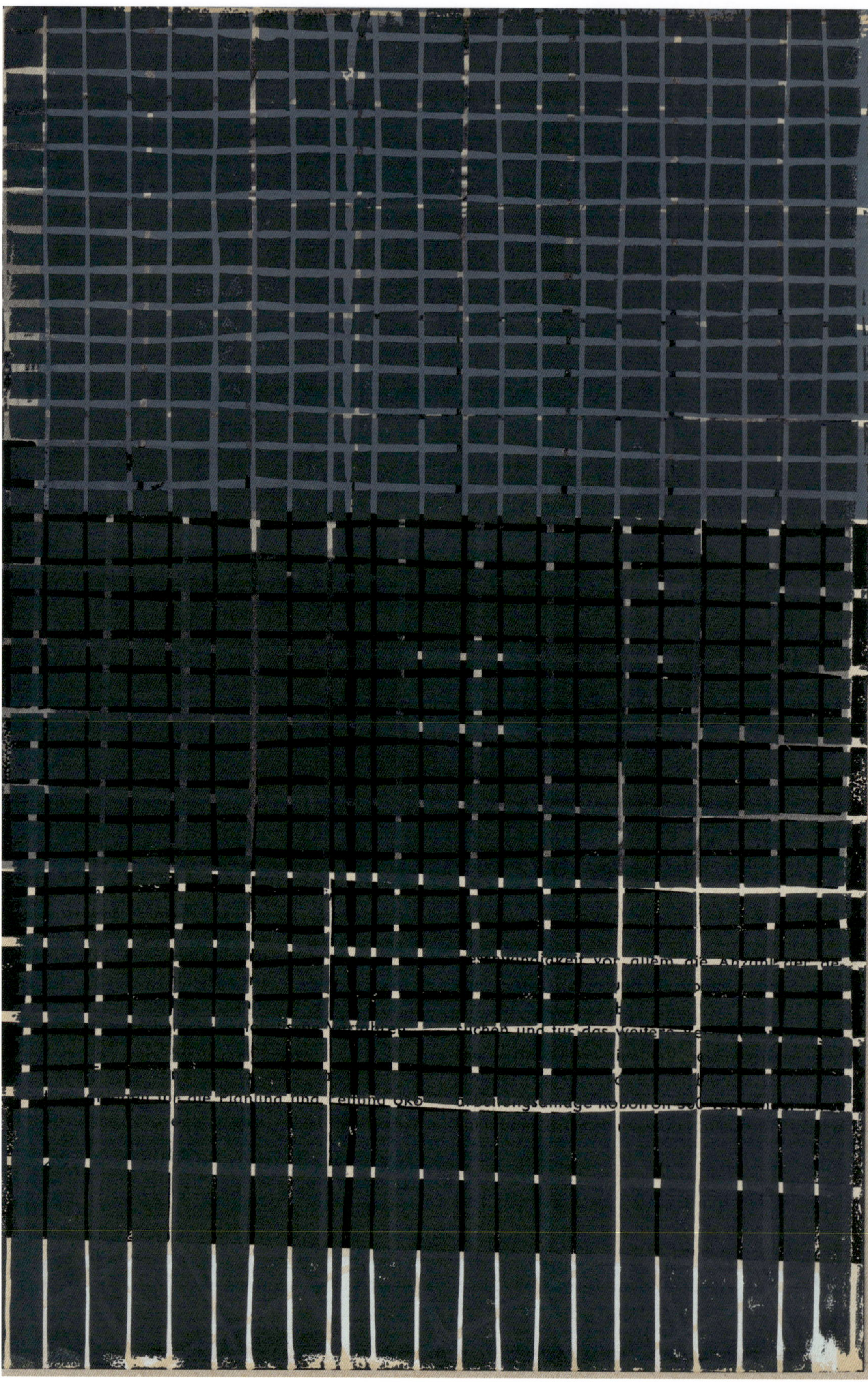

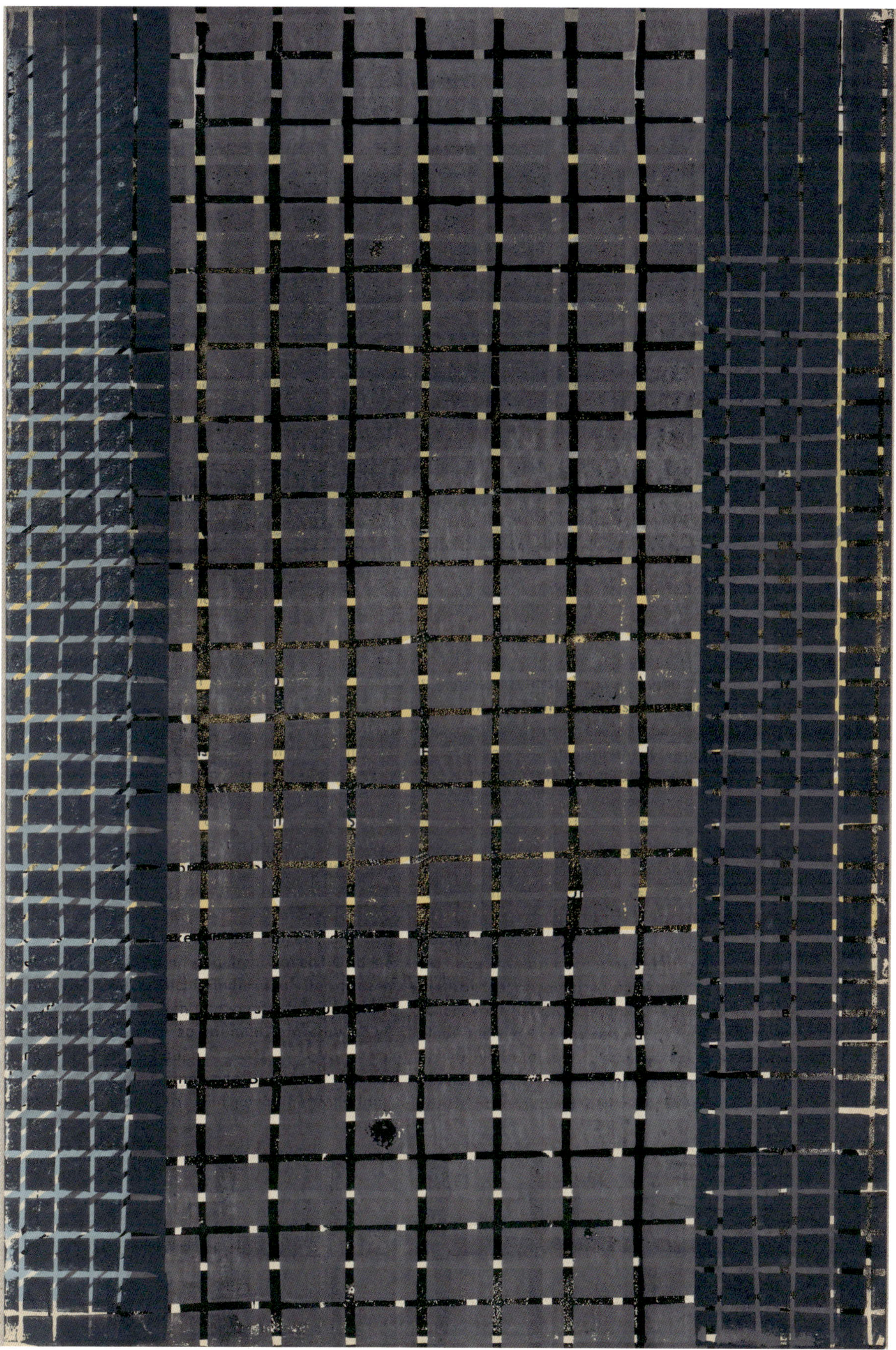

CLEARANCE SPACE

Linocut from one
plate on fine art paper
2019

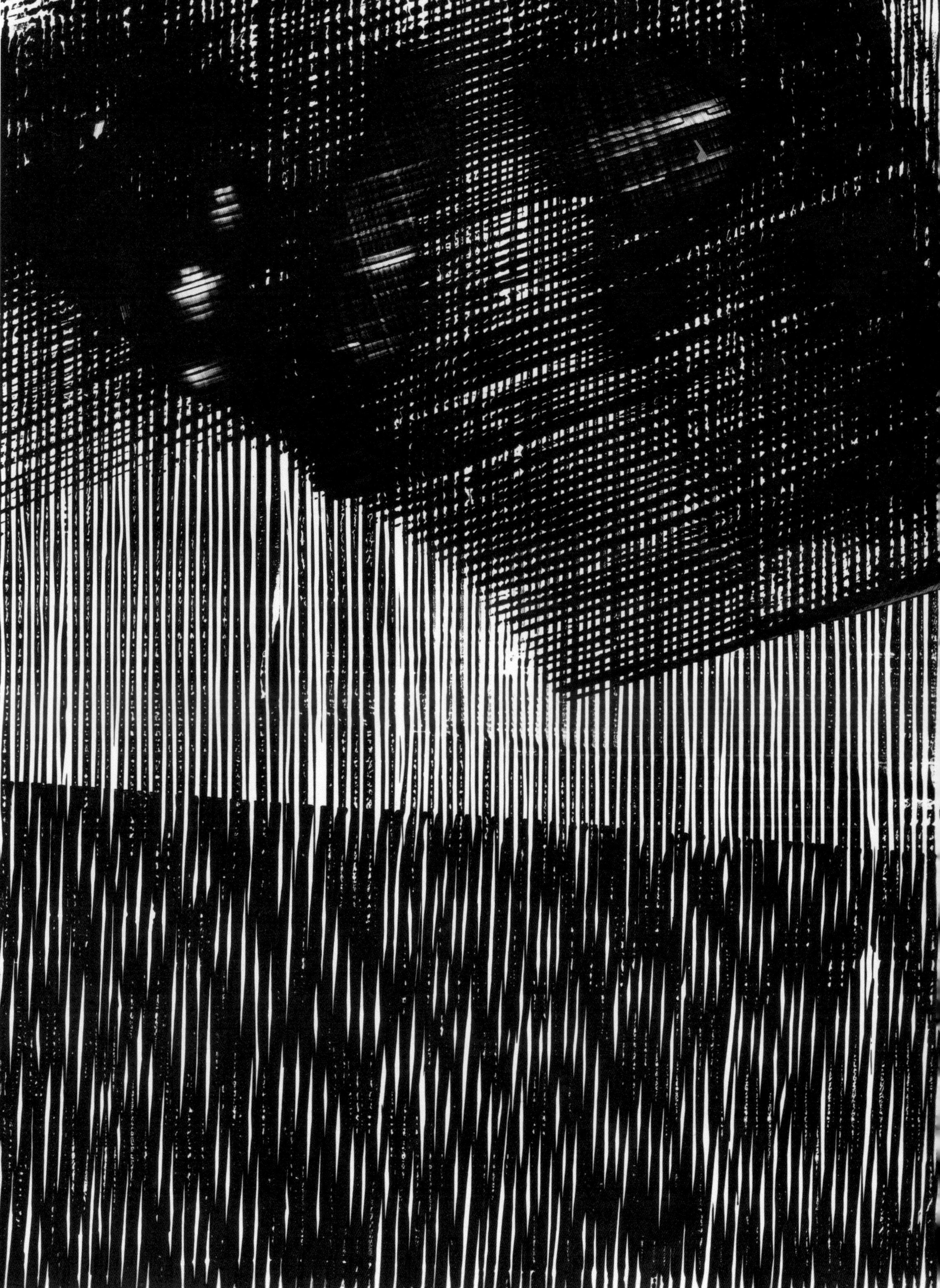

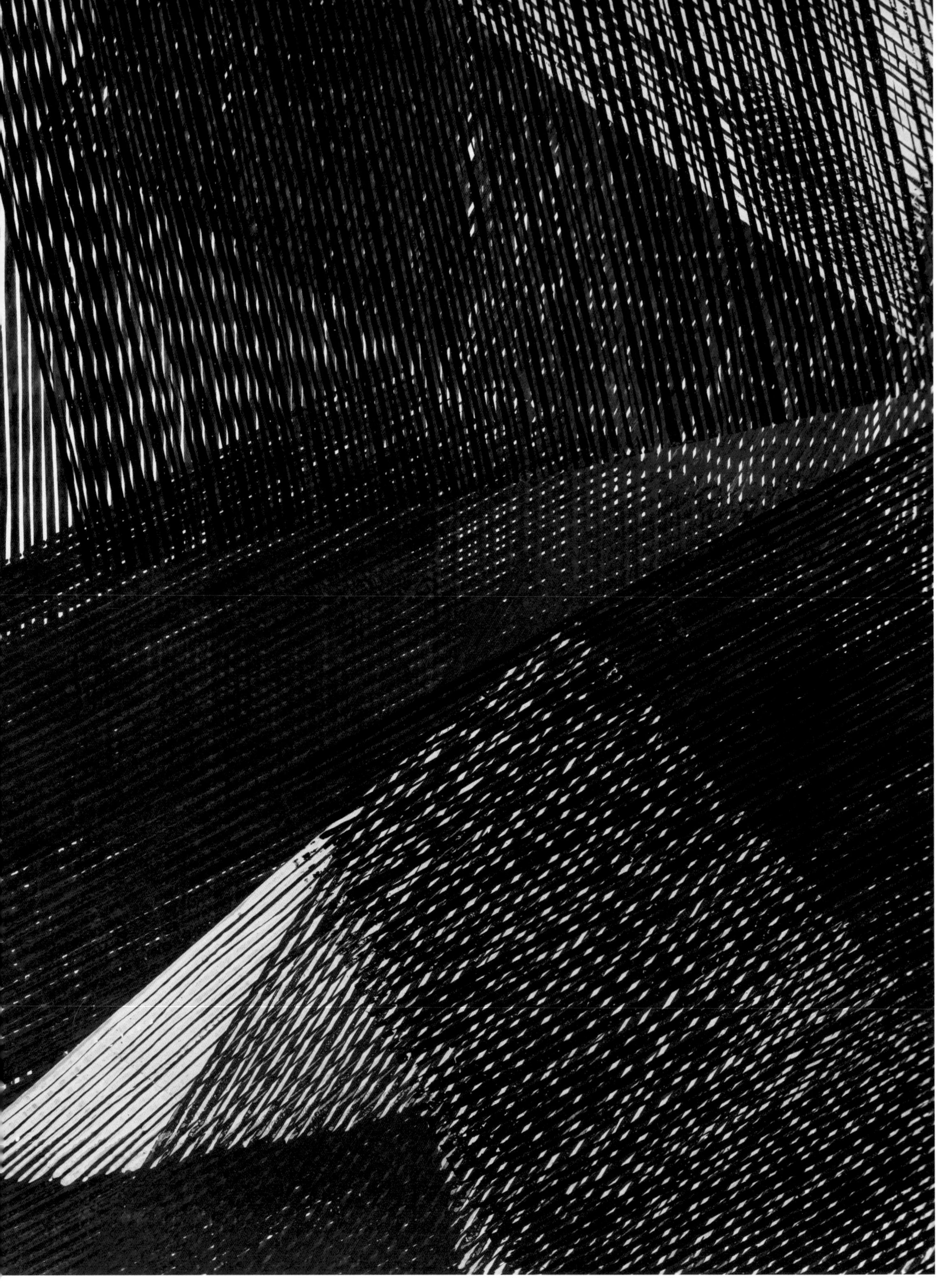

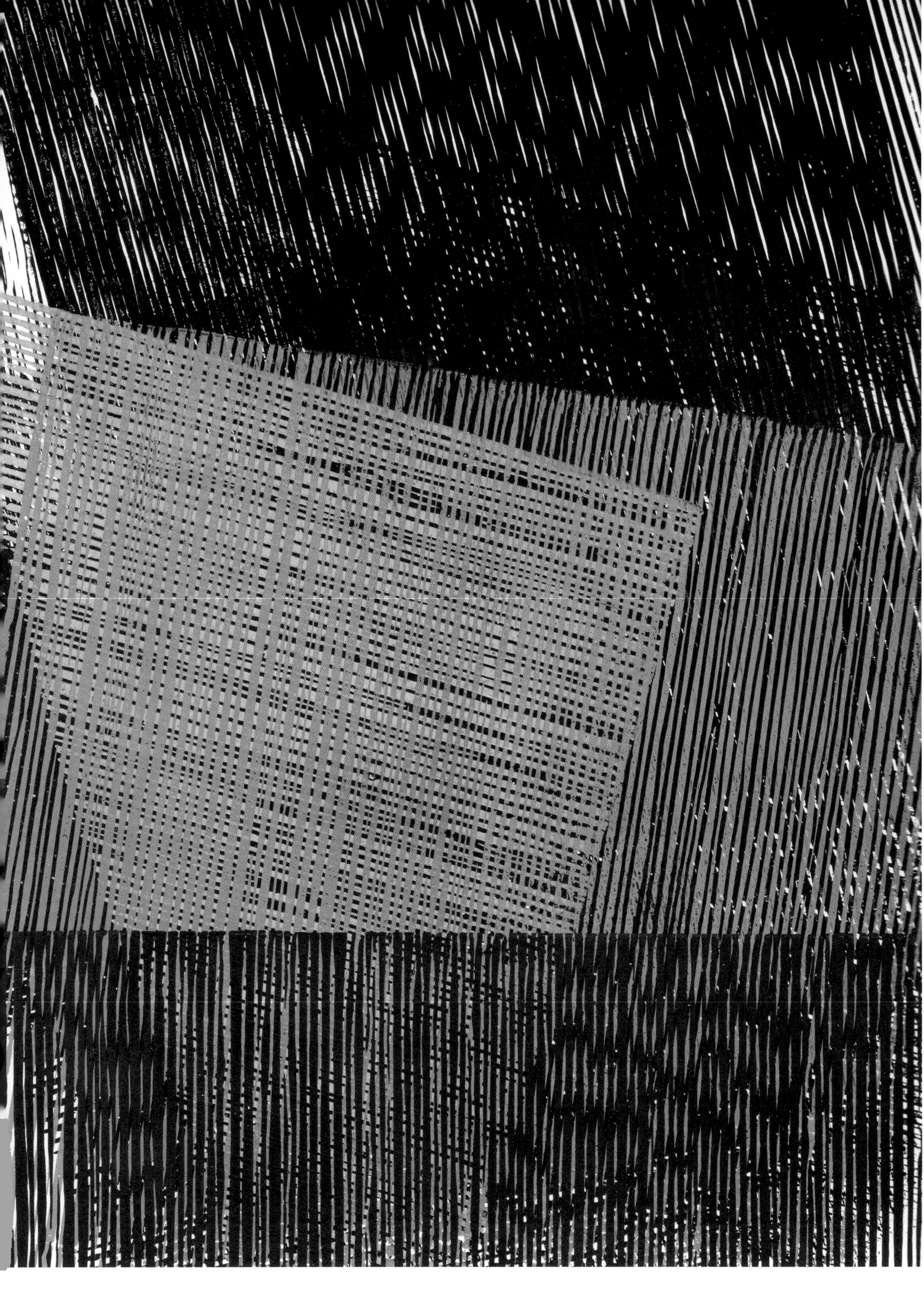

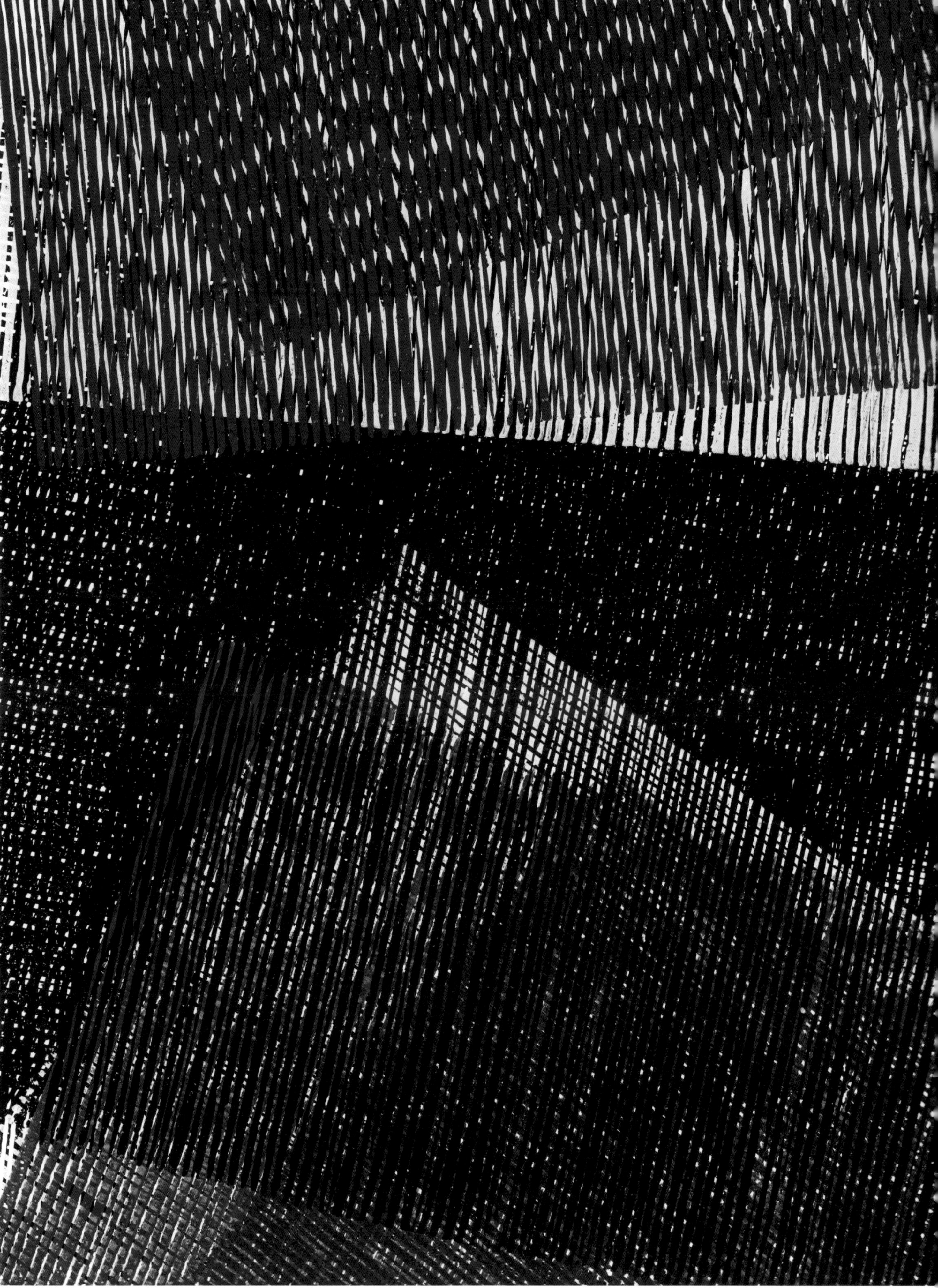

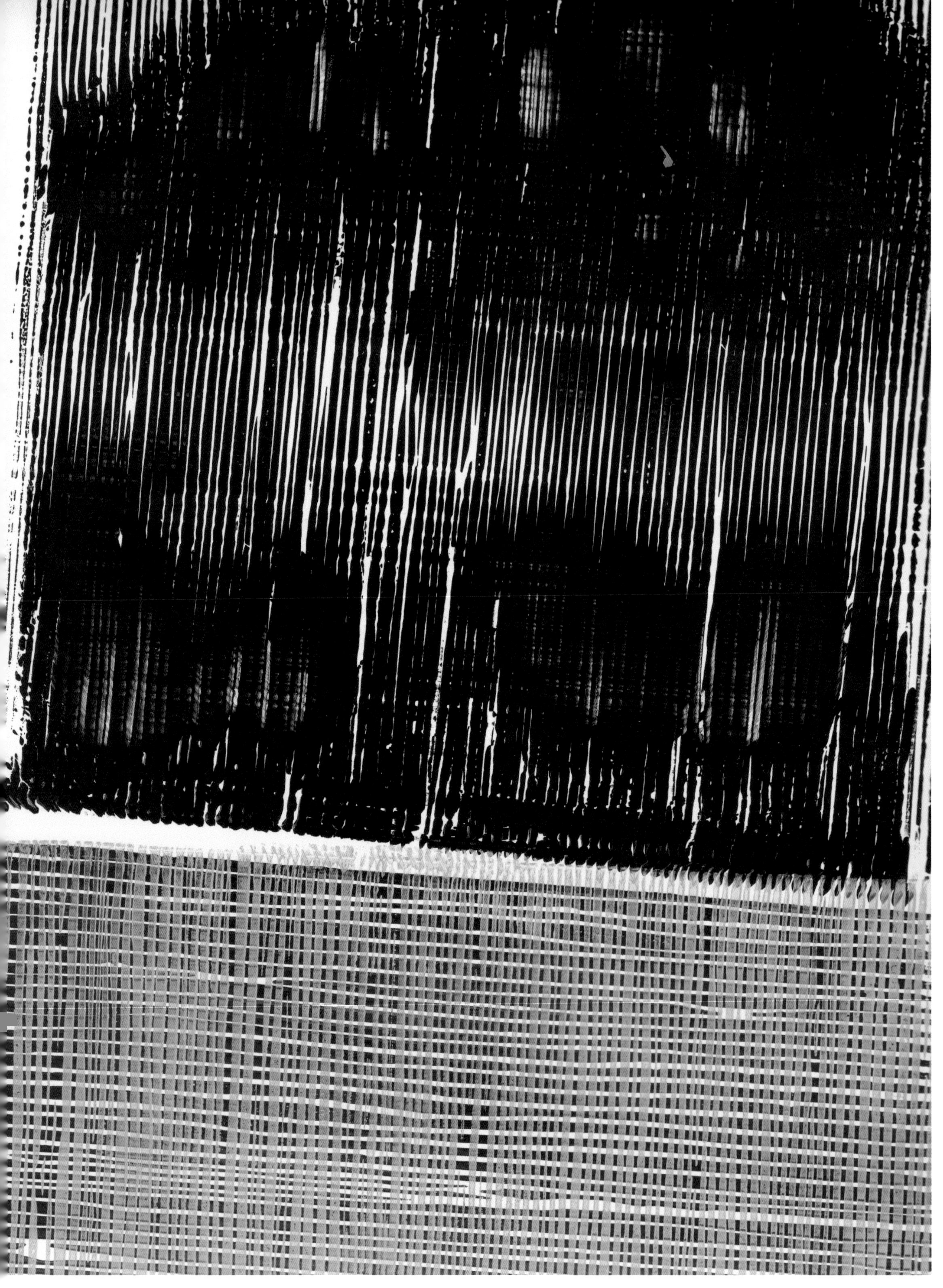

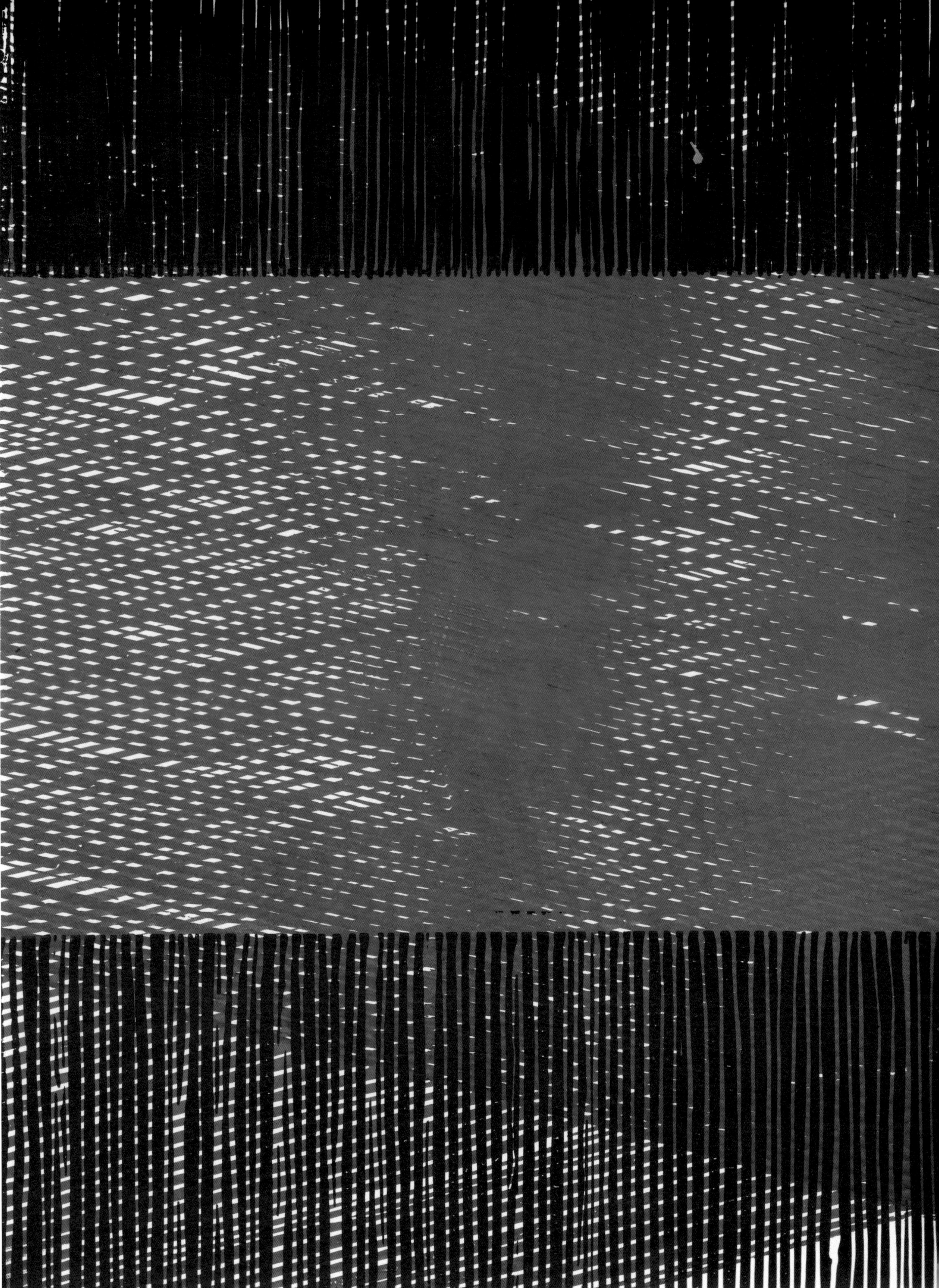

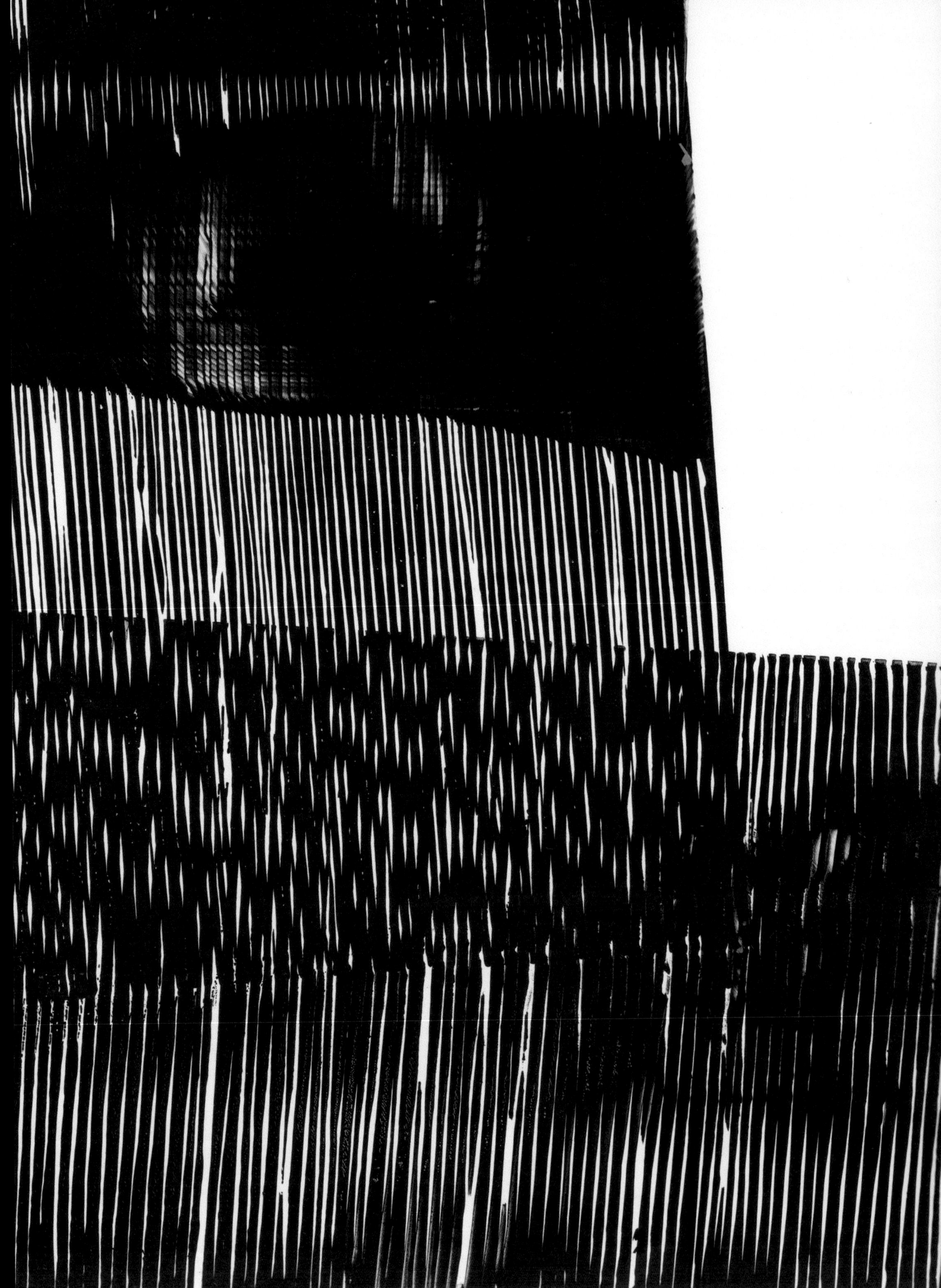

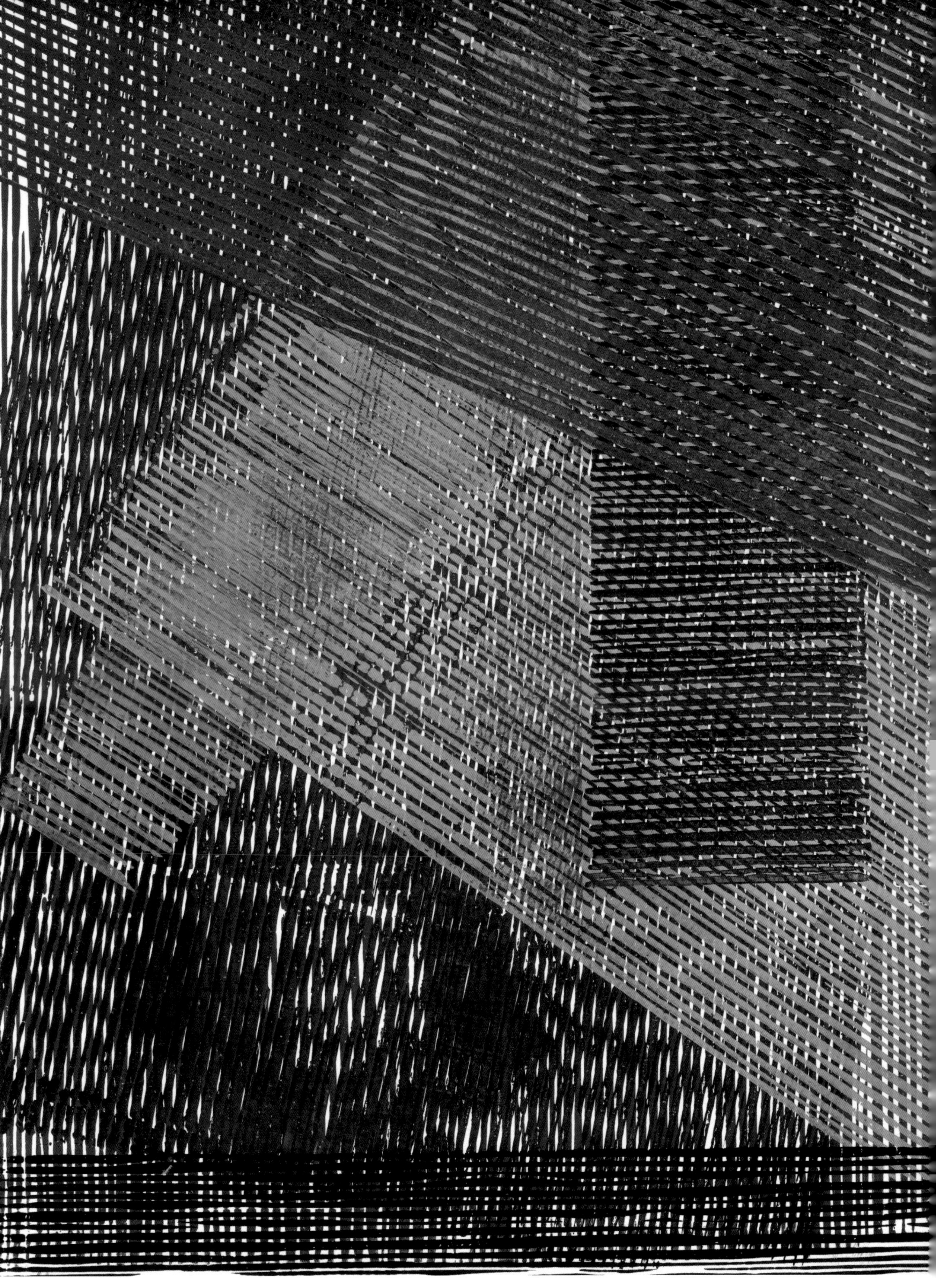

RECALLING

Video work, duration: 5:47 min
30 kg burned sand and performer on
paper, 3,66 x 4 m
2017

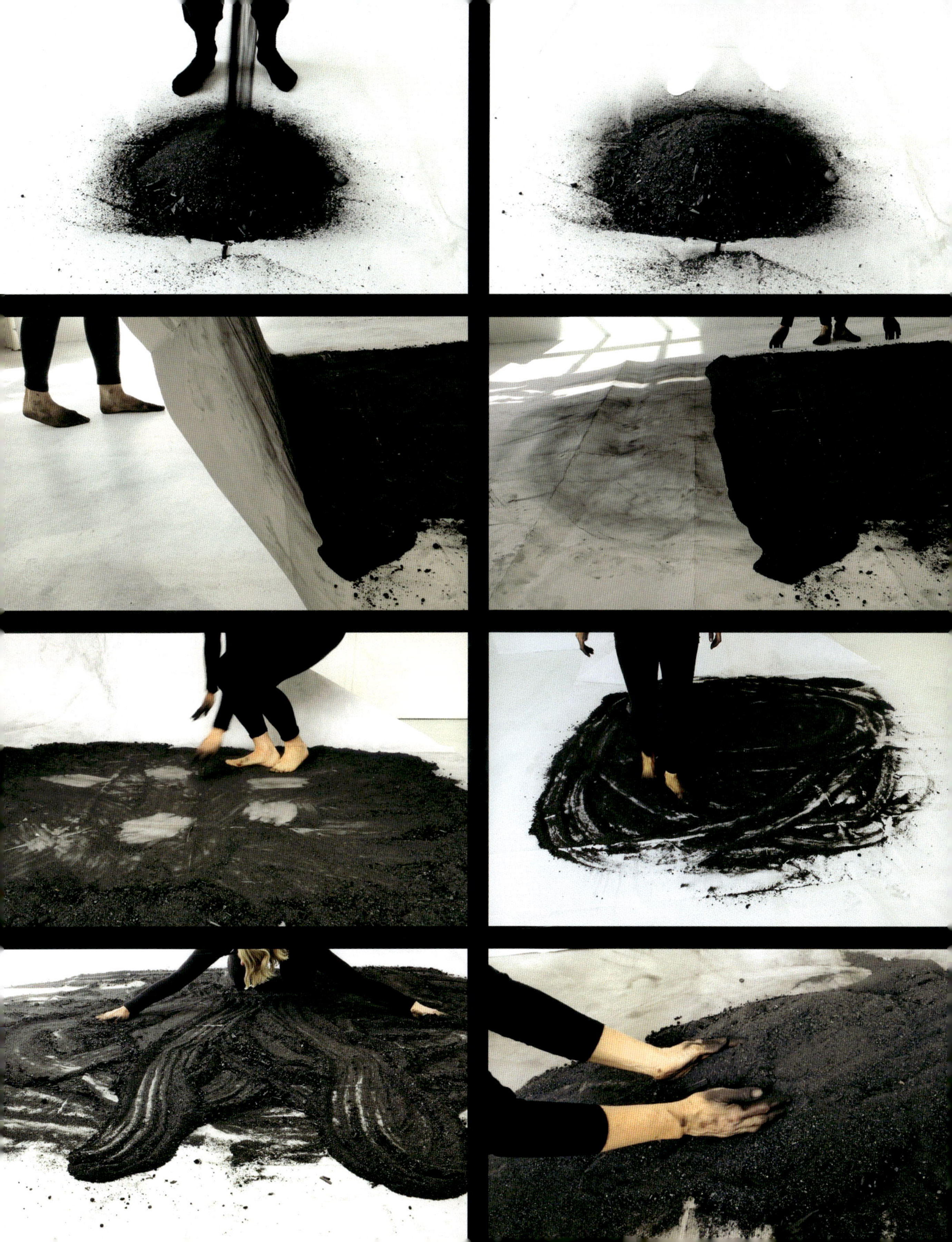

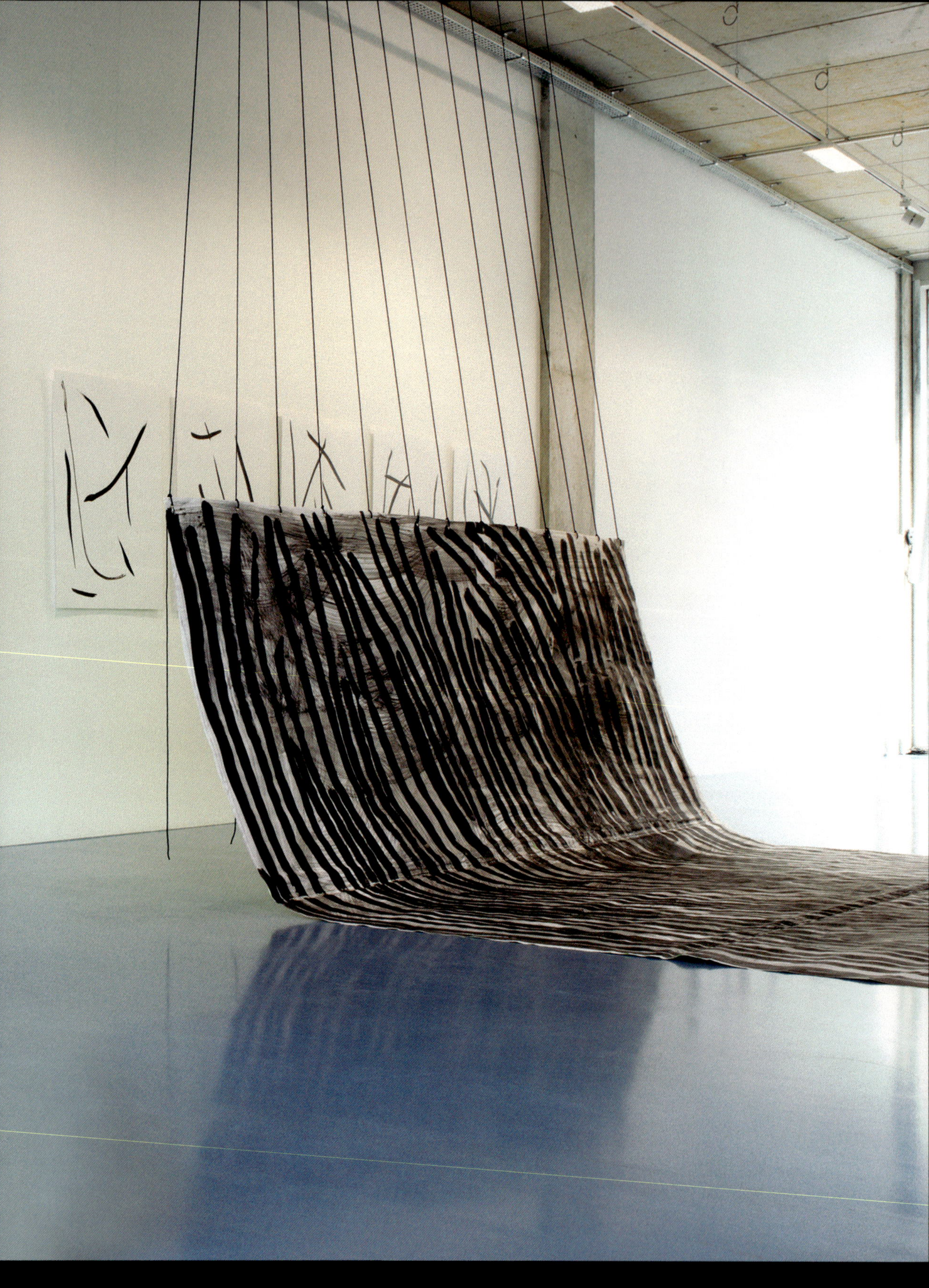

SURFACE AREAS

Installation, five drawings, ink on paper, à 84 x 119 cm
One drawing, coal, ink, acrylic paint on paper 3 x 4 m
Exhibition view, installation as a part of the group show
the horizon looks different from afar by pilote
contemporary at CLB Berlin
2019

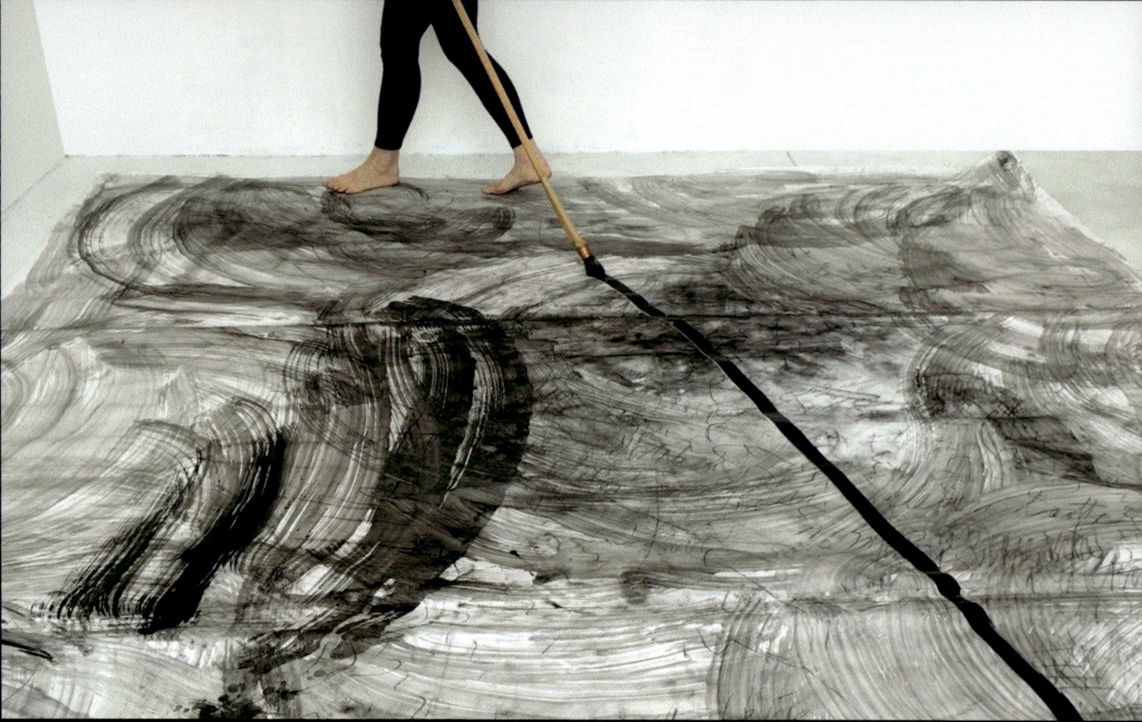

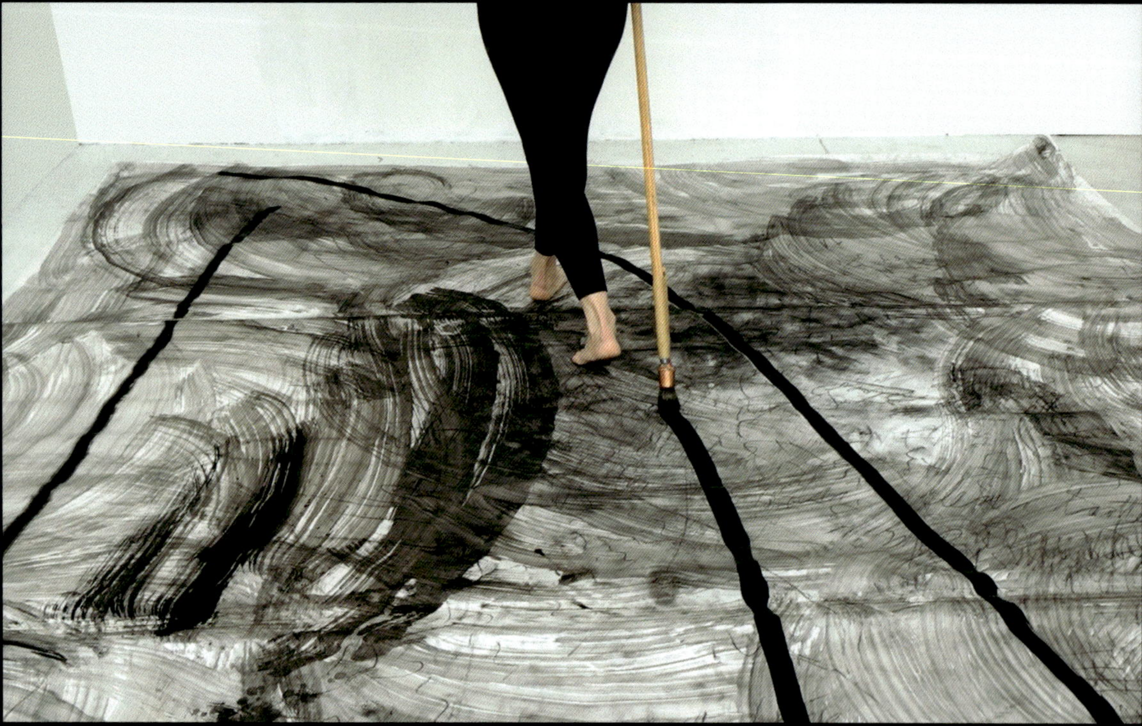

Studio views, video stills

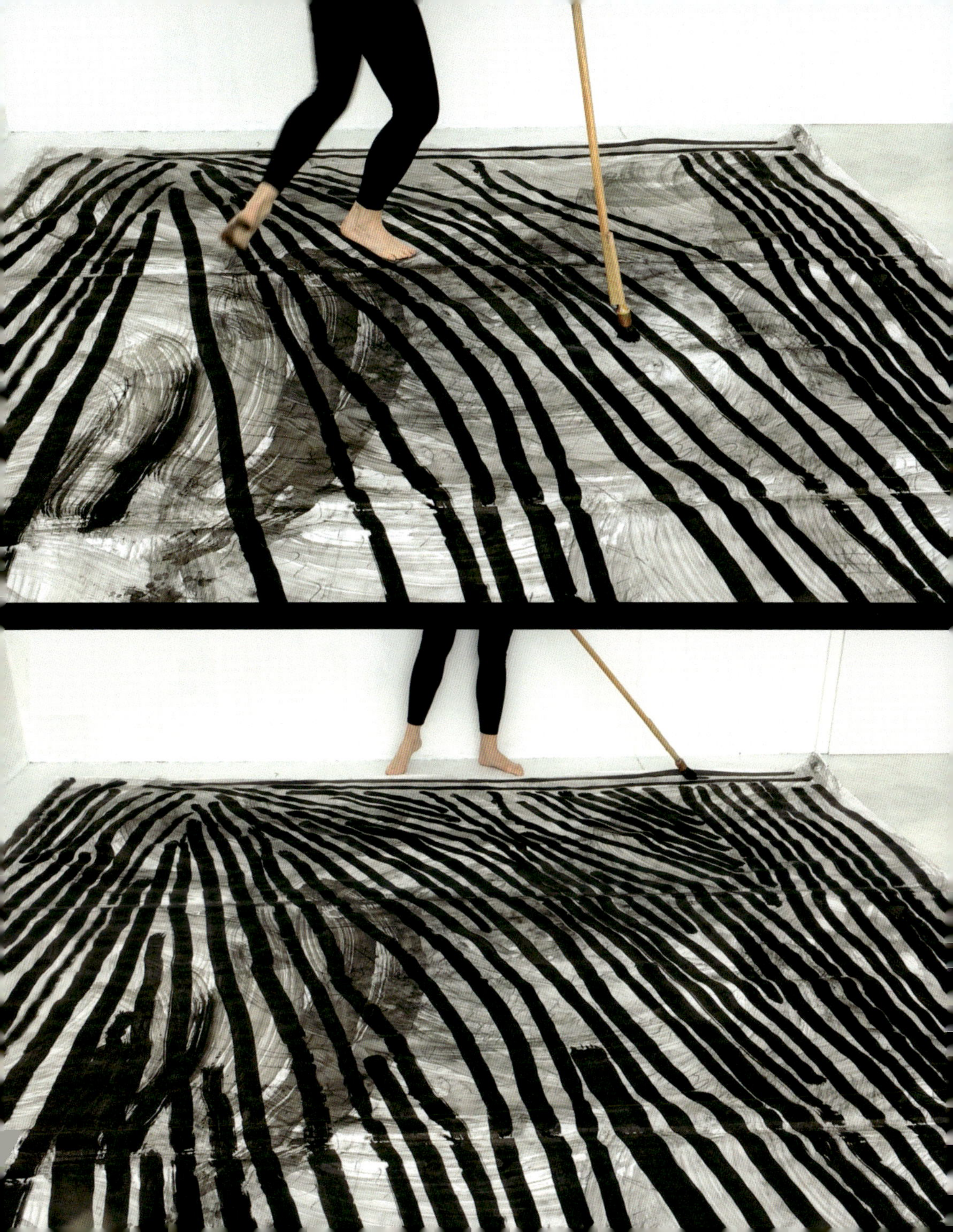

ART WORKS AS PROPOSITIONS ABOUT KNOWING

HELEN VERRAN

This reading of Katja Pudor's art work began during a visit to her studio in Berlin, which was intended as a kind of conversational ethnography with Katja and her works. Josefine Raasch, a common friend of Katja's and mine, had brought us together. On the day of our visit early in the winter of 2018, there were, then, three humans in the studio space along with many images in varying degrees of becoming art objects. In listening to, watching, and recording Katja as she moved around the space, explaining and showing, and in studying and photographing some of the images with our phones, we came to see ourselves as participants in an event, a small episode in which our lives (and our friendships) and 'doing art' collectively emerged as one and the same thing. Using the language of a twentieth-century art movement, we could call this "a blurred happening of art and life"[1]. One particular artwork still in the process of becoming helped me formulate a way to understand this experience. I refer to this work inthe conclusion.

Within my overall contention that artworks emerge from the blur where collective life and art happen, I discuss Katja's recent artworks as *propositions*. My readings of Katja's works regard them as setting forth insights into the relation of endurance and experience. The English term 'proposition' is echoed in the verb 'to propound', which means 'to put forward'. The same word root occurs in both 'expound' and 'compound', and these related terms are useful in making clear what I am suggesting. In reading these works of art as 'proposing', I am not seeing them as loudly proclaiming, nor as complicating and complexifying, but rather as quietly showing and demonstrating. Whereas art works are often read as expressions of 'the political' or 'the psychological', I find that Katja Pudor's art offers epistemic insights. I see them as interested in 'revealing' the figure of the artist as knower.

Elaborating my contention that artistic works can be visual propositions, and that what we see here are propositions concerning the relation of experience and

Abb. 1
Recalling, 2017, 30 kg burned sand and performer on paper, 3,66 × 4 m, video work, duration: 5:47 min

endurance, I begin with the somewhat underwhelming and perhaps confusing claim that experience is just experience—not experience of. Endurance, then, is a mode of experience as experience: We do not immediately experience things as 'the thing as such', that will come later when we work with words and engage in interpretation. And that is exactly what I am doing here. The philosophy of art that I encountered in Katja's studio reveals that she has learned to expand and prolong, to cultivate, that ephemeral 'space' between experiencing experience and experiencing things. Her art is inquiry into the workings of that 'space'. My contention is that the work exhibited here develops wordless propositions concerning the experience of endurance.

Proposition One. *Recalling* 2017, video

Recalling inquires into relations between experience and memories. 'Where are memories deposited?', it seems to both ask and answer. In the beginning, a large sheet of white paper. The figure of the black-clothed embodied artist pours a quantity of black burned sand; the viewer hears the sounds of the gritty sand leaving the unseen, aluminium-sounding bowl and landing on the paper. After nearly a minute, a pile almost a metre across and around 30 cm high sits in the middle of the screen. The artist walks away and the viewer is surprised to see her former presence as remembered and hence as enduring. A pair of very white footprints have formed in a just visible layer of dust. Relationally, the paper and the dust 'remember'. Keep watching; inchoate experience of experience. The artist's bare feet work their way through the black sand pile as she moves in circles; the pile flattens and spreads. The memory of the sand blackens the feet's pinkish skin; the shuffling feet are indistinctly recalled as circular tracks. In the final minute, the artist's hands scoop up handfuls, shifting sand from here to an unseen there.

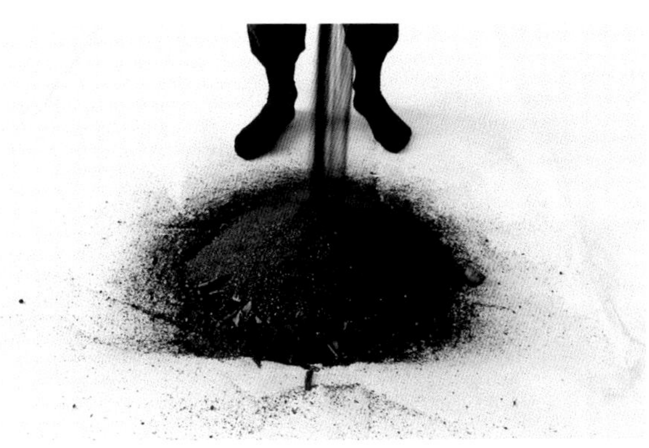
1

Imagining, I juxtapose the experience of my participation as reader of the video text and the artist's experience. She has the white paper, scrunchy black

KUNSTWERKE ALS PROPOSITIONEN ÜBER DAS WISSEN

Das Lesen von Katja Pudors Arbeiten begann während eines Besuches in Katjas Berliner Atelier, bei dem ich beabsichtigte, mit Katja und ihren Werken eine dialogorientierte Ethnografie durchzuführen. Josefine Raasch, eine gemeinsame Freundin von Katja und mir, hatte uns zusammengebracht. Am Tag unseres Besuchs im Frühwinter 2018 befanden sich also drei Menschen und viele Arbeiten in unterschiedlichen Stadien des Werdens im Atelier. Indem wir Katja zuhörten, zusahen und aufnahmen, wie sie sich im Raum bewegte, erklärend und zeigend, und indem wir uns mit ihren Bildern befassten und einige mit unseren Handys fotografierten, begannen wir, uns als Teilnehmerinnen an einem Ereignis wahrzunehmen. Es war eine kleine Episode, in der unsere Leben (und unsere Freundschaften) und das „Kunstmachen" kollektiv als ein und dieselbe Sache wahrgenommen wurden. In der Sprache einer Kunstbewegung des 20. Jahrhunderts könnten wir diese Erfahrung als ein ‚blurred happening of art and life'[1], als ein undeutliches Geschehen von Kunst und Leben bezeichnen. Eine spezifische Arbeit, die noch im Entstehen ist, hat mir dabei geholfen, zu formulieren, wie diese Erfahrung verstanden werden kann. Ich beziehe mich am Ende des Textes auf diese Arbeit.

Meine allgemeine Behauptung ausführend, dass Kunst buchstäblich aus der Unschärfe entsteht, in der sich kollektives Leben und Kunst ereignen, erörtere ich Katja Pudors jüngste Arbeiten als *Propositionen*. Meine Lesart von Katjas Arbeiten betrachtet sie als Darlegungen, die Einblicke in die

sand, and the implacable video camera recording as her companions. Not to mention the space formed by walls painted white, which form the background, and her supportive family, friends, and other social institutions, which are absent from the frame. My experience of experience as reader has quite different companions. My experience of experience endures for about six minutes; her experience in contriving the video text no doubt lasted much, much longer and might have been filled with false starts and failed attempts, as well as bothersome technical detail.

The point is that although very different, as experiences of experience, each is equally inchoate, messy, indeterminate. The artist's interpretation of her experience is the video text. The interpreter's 'reading' is the preceding paragraphs. And, let us not fail to notice that you too, as reader of these words, have experienced inchoate experience in reading. Of course, later you might experience the experience of watching the video, and you might (re)interpret the experiences of reading and watching.

Proposition Two. *Surface Areas* 2019, installation

Burrowing in to see the proposition is trickier here. As I read the juxtapositional display, in this work the proposition takes the form of an injunction: "Experience endurance!". The would-be reader meets two sets of surface areas. The one, a large surface area hanging vertically and lying horizontally is densely covered with line. The second consists of five sheets of white paper with five black lines on each. The display collected together in this book offers two glimpses of these sheets of paper at different stages of the 'doing of art': on the wall of a gallery subject to the scrutiny of the artwork's viewers, and on the floor of the studio in the process of becoming. In the first thumbnail, this juxtaposition of sets of surface areas is seen as two art works juxtaposed.

The dual sets of surface areas propose two distinct modes for obeying the injunction: "Experience endurance!". To distinguish these modes, however, we need to intensify our understanding of the workings of the space, which connects experience as experience and experience of nameable things. We need to separate out our experiencing experience mediated with words and visuals, and experiencing experience mediated solely by visuals. American Pragmatist philosopher C.S. Peirce formulated a descriptive typology that we can use to tease these apart. He described differing logics of semiotic materialising, alternative ways that things, the 'stuff' of the

---

Beziehung zwischen Geduld oder vom Aushalten des Noch-Unklaren und der schließlich gemachten Erfahrung anbieten. Der englische Begriff „Proposition" kommt im Verb „vorschlagen" (to propound) vor und bedeutet „hervorbringen" (to put forward). Derselbe Wortstamm kommt sowohl in „darlegen" (expound) als auch in „zusammensetzen" (compound) vor. Diese verwandten Begriffe sind nützlich, um zu verdeutlichen, worauf ich hinweisen möchte. Wenn ich diese Arbeiten als „vorschlagend" beschreibe, sehe ich sie nicht als lautstark proklamierend, verkomplizierend und komplexer machend, sondern eher als leise zeigend und veranschaulichend. Während Kunst oft als Ausdruck des „Politischen" oder des „Psychologischen" gelesen wird, finde ich, dass Katja Pudors Arbeiten erkenntnistheoretische Einsichten vermitteln. Ich begreife sie als Werke, die die Figur der Künstler*in als Wissende*r „offenlegen" wollen.

Meine Annahmen weiter ausführend, dass künstlerische Arbeiten visuelle Propositionen sein könnten und das, was wir hier sehen, Propositionen über das Verhältnis von Erfahrung und Geduld / Aushalten sind, beginne ich mit der wohl nicht gerade überwältigenden und etwas verwirrenden Behauptung, dass Erfahrung nur Erfahrung ist – nicht Erfahrung von etwas. Aushalten ist also ein Modus der Erfahrung als Erfahrung: Wir erleben Dinge nicht unmittelbar als „Ding an sich"; das kommt erst, wenn wir mit Sprache arbeiten und uns mit Interpretationen auseinandersetzen. Und genau das mache ich hier. Die Philosophie, der ich in Katjas Atelier begegnet bin, zeigt, dass sie gelernt hat, diesen vergänglichen „Raum" zwischen Erfahren und Erfahren von Dingen zu erweitern, zu verlängern und zu kultivieren. Ihre Kunst ist die die Untersuchung der Gestaltung dieses „Raumes". Meine Behauptung ist, dass die hier gezeigte Arbeit

Abb. 2
Surface Areas, 2019, different medias on paper, installation as a part of the group show *the horizon looks different from afar*

Abb. 3
Surface Areas, 2019, first series of five series, studio view, ink on five different papers

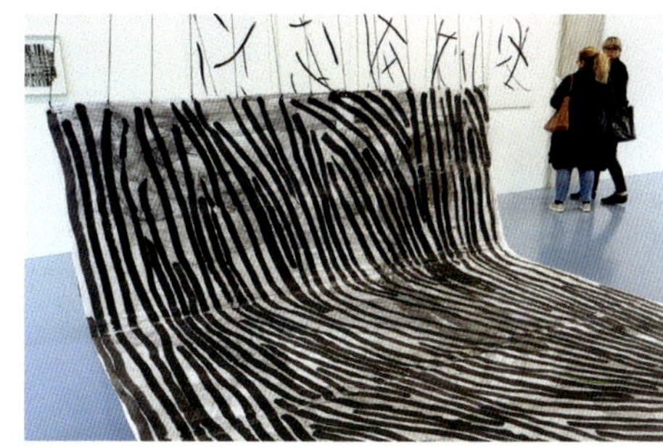
2

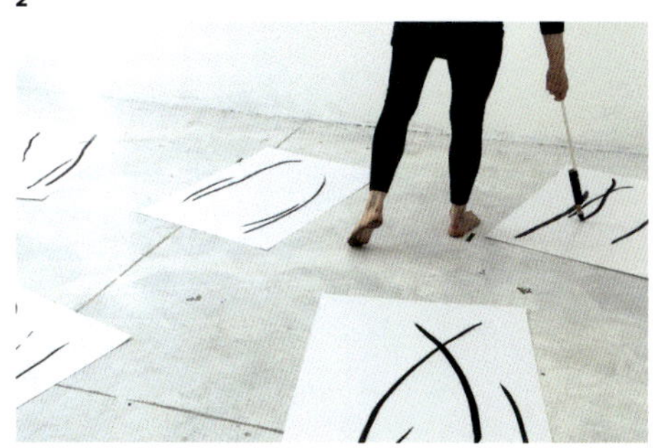
3

world, might become meaningful. Using this typology, we can make a distinction between the two sets of surface areas.

Symbolising requires words and visuals, and I see the large surface area dense with line, hanging vertically / lying horizontally as symbolising. I think landscape and three dimensions; a passage from horizontal to vertical. But I must think in words to get there. In contrast, five sheets of white paper, shown here on the wall of a gallery and there on the floor of a studio, together index the collective action of a long-handled brush, black ink in a plastic cup, an artist walking in circles, here lifting an ink-laden brush, there lowering it. No words are required to experience experience, but we must imagine the collective action. Perhaps we can say that the one art object symbolises spatial endurance, the other indexes temporal endurance. Different endurances are experienced.

Proposition Three. *Urania Universum* 2018, linocut
Urania Universum was a popular journal during the communist years in East Germany, published annually by the press Urania Verlag, Leipzig between 1955 and 1990. Focusing on global scientific and cultural developments, it featured scientific, sporting, technical, and cultural accomplishments of this totalitarian regime, setting them in a global frame.

Volume 14 was published in 1968 in East Germany, a year of memorable politics for many in Germany, East and West. For Katja, who was born in the GDR, the book was important as it was published in a year made memorable by the birth of her brother. Katja was not one of those who read the pages of this volume in 1968, but perhaps she remembers reading them years later, when the events of that year were already collective memory. Perhaps she remembers enough of her childhood, the people she lived amongst, and the places she lived in for the first twenty years of her life, to vividly imagine these pages being read in 1968.

---

wortlose Propositionen über das Erleben von Aushalten entwickelt.

Proposition Eins. *Recalling* 2017, Video
Recalling fragt nach Beziehungen zwischen Erfahrungen und Erinnerungen. „Wo sind Erinnerungen gelagert?“, scheint die Arbeit zu fragen und zu beantworten. Am Anfang ein großes weißes Blatt Papier. Die Gestalt der schwarz gekleideten Künstlerin schüttet eine große Menge schwarz gebrannten Sand aus: Die Betrachter*in der Bilder hört die Geräusche des kiesigen Sandes, als er die unsichtbare, nach Aluminium klingende Schüssel verlässt und auf dem Papier landet. Nach fast einer Minute bildet der Sand eine Anhäufung mit einem Durchmesser von fast einem Meter und einer Höhe von dreißig Zentimetern in der Mitte des Bildschirms. Die Künstlerin geht weg und die Betrachter*in ist überrascht, dass ihre vorherige Anwesenheit in Erinnerung bleibt und somit andauert. Ein Paar weißer Fußabdrücke zeichnet sich in einer fast unsichtbaren Staubschicht ab. Im relationalen Sinne ‚erinnern‘ sich Papier und Staub. Schauen Sie weiter hin; eine unfertige Erfahrung der Erfahrung. Die nackten Füße der Künstlerin arbeiten sich durch den schwarzen Sandhaufen, während sie sich in Kreisen bewegt; die Anhäufung flacht ab und breitet sich aus. Die Erinnerung an den Sand schwärzt die rosafarbene Haut der Füße; als kreisförmige Spuren bleiben die gleitenden Füße undeutlich in Erinnerung. Gegen Ende der Performance schöpfen die Hände der Künstlerin Sand aus dem Hier zu einem nicht sichtbaren Dort.

Proposition Zwei. *Surface Areas* 2019, Installation
In meiner Vorstellung stelle ich die Erfahrung meiner Teilnahme als Leser*in des Videotexts und die Erfahrung der Künstler*in nebeneinander. Das weiße Papier, der knirschende schwarze Sand

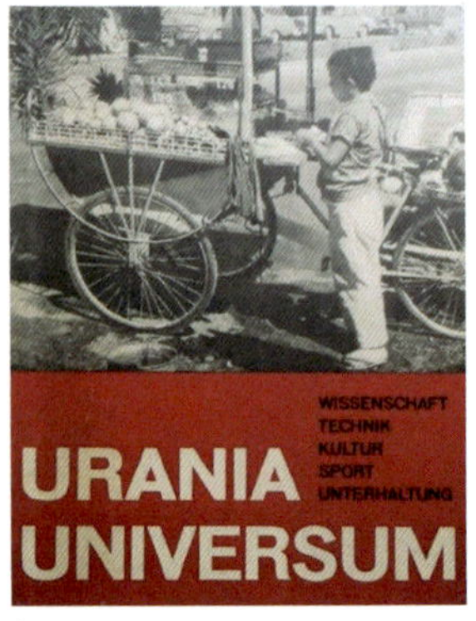

4

Abb. 4

Cover Urania Universum, screenshot, https://www.buchfreund.de/de/d/p/ 87939777/urania-universum-band-14

What might a young East German girl make of the image of the boy selling(?) fruits from his bicycle cart? And what of the rest of the information: "Wissenschaft, Technik, Kultur, Sport [und] Unterhaltung", that lay between the covers, no doubt conforming to and expressing the cultural policies ofthe regime?

The words and images collected together and published in the journal in 1968 expressed the collective life in a particular time and place, and in 2018 it endures in book form, lurking in second-hand book stores. But how does one read and experience this in Berlin in 2018? The series of images that constitute the artwork *Urania Universum* offers up a proposition on the relation between experience and endurance in response to that question. The thumbnail image on the left is Katja Pudor's answer to that question with respect to page 480 of *Urania Universum*, volume 14, which you see on the right. The artistexperiences words read and expressed this experience: in several steps and with several printing plates, the original page was over-printed. We who study the image that page 479 has become read not words, but colours—pale blue and black and white, intersecting lines, and the shapes they generate. Just a little of the original remains salient as a background of faded pinkish-brown paper of poor quality.

What is our experience, those of us who read the images generated in this process? Here we have options. We might confine our experience to the visual, all the while recognising that, invisible beneath the layers of paint that have been printed onto the paper, there are words that once were meaningful to many people. Or we might pay close attention to the artist's process and, to some extent, mimic her experience by taking time to read carefully the words on the back of the image; we might read page 480 and study the image that page 479 has become.

We can feel ourselves *experiencing non-endurance* in attending to this artwork. Taking up the first option, we have the possibility of experiencing this non-endurance as a vague, whole obliteration. The second option, accessed by taking some time to 'do our homework' as the cultural theorist Gayatri Spivak[2] would say, helps us to 'colour-in' this vague sense of obliteration; to experience it in its weird minutiae. Let us start to read at the top of page 480. Carrying on from the now unreadable words of page 479, our topic is clearly science and technology in architecture of

---

und die unerbittlich aufzeichnende Kamera sind ihre Begleiter*innen; ebenso wie der Raum aus weiß gestrichenen Wänden, die den Hintergrund bilden,und ihre Familie, die sie unterstützt, ihre Freunde und andere sozialen Einrichtungen, die in diesem Rahmen fehlen. Meine Erfahrung der Erfahrung als Leser*in hat ganz andere Begleiter*innen. Meine Erfahrung der Erfahrung dauert ungefähr sechs Minuten; ihre Erfahrung des Inszenierens und Produzierens des Videotexts hat zweifellos viel länger angehalten und war womöglich von Fehlstarts, missglückten Versuchen und lästigen technischen Details geprägt.

Obwohl beide, als Erfahrungen der Erfahrung, sehr unterschiedlich sind, ist jede für sich gleichermaßen unfertig, chaotisch und unbestimmt. Im Videotext interpretiert die Künstlerin ihre Erfahrungen, deren Auslegung spielt sich in den vorhergehenden Absätzen ab. Und natürlich haben auch Sie, als Leser*in dieser Zeilen, eine unfertige Erfahrungen beim Lesen gemacht. Möglichweise machen Sie die Erfahrung des Betrachtens des Videos später und interpretieren daraufhin die Erfahrungen des Lesens und Betrachtens neu.

In dieser Arbeit sind die Proposition schwieriger zu erkennen. Während ich die nebeneinanderstehenden Bilder lese, formt sich die Proposition in dieser Arbeit zu einer Anweisung: „Erfahre das Aushalten!" Die*der potenzielle Leser*in trifft auf zwei Gruppen von Oberflächen. Die erste, eine große Fläche, die vertikal hängt und horizontal liegt, ist dicht mit Linien bedeckt. Die zweite besteht aus fünf weißen Blättern mit jeweils fünf schwarzen Linien. Die in diesem Buch zusammengestellte Präsentation bietet zwei kurze Blicke auf diese Zeichnungen in verschiedenen Stadien des „Kunstmachens": an der Wand einer Galerie, wo sie der gründlichen Betrachtung der Besucher*innen ausgesetzt sind und auf dem Boden

Abb. 5

Urania Universum #25, 2018, linocut from multiple plates on book page, 23,5 × 15,5 cm

Abb. 6

Urania Universum Band 14, Seite 480

5

6

the world of 1968. The unknown author of these words has used a quotation from a talk given in 1941, in the midst of World War II, by Albert Einstein, winner of a Nobel Prize in physics nearly twenty years before.

> *(…) a new way to build apartments, a new way to build factories and offices and a new idea of beauty that corresponded to the possibility of the new technology. But then came World War II, and with it, the collapse of all conception of perfecting the capitalistic world through technology. Einstein's judgement of this capitalistic world was that it wielded the „highest perfection of means, highest confusion of the goals".*[3]

Perhaps readers in East Germany in 1968 were familiar with this quotation? Maybe it was common knowledge back then that the famous physicist ends the talk from which this quotation is taken with these words concerning the goal of applying the 'one and only' correct method for discerning the so-called laws of the physical world:

> *Even if only a small part of mankind strives for such goals, their superiority will prove itself in the long run.*[4]

How do I know the ending of the quotation at the top of page 480? This being neither 1941 nor 1968, I googled it and found a YouTube video of Einstein delivering his speech in English. In 2019, watching and listening to Einstein pompously speaking as a prophet in 1941, the rightness of Katja Pudor's art on page 479 registered with force; with a knowing embodied certainty.

Temporally speaking, *Urania Universum* partially transfers our gaze back to the 1960s. And so too did a becoming work of art that I encountered very soon after I walked into Katja Pudor's studio in Berlin in December 2018. A particular set of English words written in a seemingly endless variety of handwriting styles, using many different types of inscription devices, caught my attention. Using my phone as recording device, I read out loud the words I can identify. From this recording I will later identify the precise origin of the words, which Katja tells us are taken from "the manifesto by Allan Kaprow". It is the 1966 *Manifesto* of the inventor

---

des Studios, wo sie im Prozess des Werdens sind. In **Abb. 2** erscheint diese Nebeneinanderstellung von verschiedenen Oberflächen als zwei nebeneinander gestellte Kunstwerke und nicht als eine Arbeit.

Diese zwei Oberflächen bringen zwei unterschiedliche Modi für die Befolgung der Anweisung „Erfahre das Aushalten!" hervor. Um diese Modi zu unterscheiden, müssen wir jedoch unser Verständnis für die Funktionsweisen jenes Raums vertiefen, der Erfahrung als Erfahrung mit Erfahrung von benennbaren Dingen verbindet. Wir müssen unser Erfahren der durch Worte und Bilder vermittelten Erfahrung von der Erfahrung, die ausschließlich durch Visuelles vermittelt erfahren wird, trennen. Der amerikanische Pragmatist C.S. Peirce formulierte eine beschreibende Typologie, mit der wir diese voneinander trennen können. Er beschrieb unterschiedliche Logiken des semiotischen Materialisierens, alternative Möglichkeiten, durch die Dinge, das „Zeug" der Welt, bedeutungsvoll werden könnten. Anhand dieser Typologie können wir den Unterschied zwischen den zwei Oberflächen treffen.

Das Symbolisieren erfordert Worte und Bilder und ich sehe die große Fläche, die dicht mit Linien bemalt ist und vertikal hängt / horizontal liegt, als symbolisierend. Mir kommen Landschaft und drei Dimensionen in den Sinn; ein Übergang von horizontal zu vertikal.

Aber ich muss in Worten denken, um dorthin zu gelangen. Im Gegensatz dazu deuten fünf weiße Blätter, die hier an der Wand einer Galerie und dort auf dem Boden eines Ateliers gezeigt werden, auf die kollektive Handlung eines langstieligen Pinsels, schwarze Tinte in einem Plastikbecher und einer Künstlerin, die im Kreis geht, einen mit Tinte getränkten Pinsel hier hebend und dort senkend. Es sind keine Worte erforderlich, um Erfahrungen zu erfahren, aber wir müssen uns

But obviously this is not the issue. The contemporary. The contemporary artist is not out to supplant recent modern art with a better kind; he wonders what art might be.

wish simply

to think in multi intermedia, overlays, fusions and juxtapositions, is a closer parallel to modern daily life than we have

attesting to our new jargon, and to our paraphernalia

electronic contact with one

found

Allan Kaprow – Manifesto

Speculative, professional philosophy of the twentieth century has generally removed itself from problems of human conduct and purpose, and plays instead a delicate role as professional activity. It could aptly be called philosophy for philosophy's sake.

Hitherto it is a commonplace

That to bring such acts and thoughts to the gallery, museum, concert hall, stage or a serious bookshop, blunts the power inherent in a art of paradoxes,

may be

is art – whether or not

or other.

nature of art today. Conflict with the past automatically one, attesting not to talent for a specialized skill

Abb. 7
Writing. A Manifesto #2, 2018, ink on paper, 100 cm x 70 cm

of the Californian art-life happenings of the late 1950s and early 1960s. I find the words on page 82 of a book published in 1993, which

> *[…] grew out of a retrospective "exhibition" of Allan Kaprow's Happenings […] For all their art-world infamy the Happenings […] were attended/experienced by relatively few. But […] what had begun as works of avant-garde art had become by 1966 […] life itself. The Happenings soon became a species of mythology […] Hoping to prolong his experiment into the meanings of everyday life Kaprow reconciled himself to letting go of the avant-garde genre.*[5]

Writing a manifesto in 1966 seems to be the means by which Kaprow contrived his 'reconciliation' with his own fame as an artist. Here is my sampling of the paragraphs which I was able to identify in Katja's rewritten manifesto:

> *What makes identifying oneself as an artist iconic is attestation […] to a philosophical stance before elusive alternatives of not-quite art and not-quite life […]*
> *Although it is commonplace to bring such acts and thought to the gallery […] to do so blunts the power inherent in an arena of paradoxes […] it evokes a history of cultural expectations that run counter to the poignant and absurd nature of art today …*
> *[…] Contemporary artists are not out to supplant recent modern art with a better kind; they wonder what art might be. Art and life are not simply commingled; the identity of each is uncertain. To pose these questions in the form of acts that are neither and both art-like nor lifelike while locating them in the framed context of the conventional showplace is to suggest that there really are no uncertainties at all. The name on the gallery or stage door [or book cover] assures us that whatever is contained within is art, and everything else is life.*
> *Precisely because art can be confused with life, it forces attention upon the aim of its ambiguities, to „reveal" experience*[6].

And Katja said about making that work:

> *For me, two things are important. I understand more and more the [meanings] of the text as I go through with hand-writing, again and again, and I think what the text is saying. And then it is the texture of that text [on the paper] when it is written by hand.*

---

das kollektive Handeln vorstellen. Vielleicht können wir sagen, dass die eine Arbeit das räumliche Aushalten symbolisiert und die andere auf das zeitliche Aushalten hindeutet. Wir erfahren unterschiedliche Arten des Aushaltens.

Proposition Drei. *Urania Universum* 2018, Softvinyldruck auf Buchseiten

Urania Universum war ein populärwissenschaftliches Jahrbuch, das während der sozialistischen Jahre in Ostdeutschland zwischen 1955 und 1990 vom Urania Verlag, Leipzig, herausgegeben wurde. Den Schwerpunkt auf globale wissenschaftliche und kulturelle Entwicklungen legend, stellte es wissenschaftliche, sportliche, technische und kulturelle Errungenschaften des totalitären Regimes heraus und setzte diese in einen globalen Rahmen.

Band 14 erschien im Jahr 1968 in Ostdeutschland, einem Jahr, das für viele Deutsche im Osten wie im Westen politisch unvergessen blieb. Für die in der DDR geborene Katja Pudor war das Buch wichtig, weil es in dem Jahr publiziert wurde, in dem ihr Bruder geboren wurde. Katja gehörte nicht zu denjenigen, die 1968 die Seiten dieses Bandes gelesen haben, aber vielleicht erinnert sie sich, sie Jahre später gelesen zu haben, als die Ereignisse dieses Jahres bereits kollektive Erinnerung waren. Vielleicht erinnert sie sich an Details ihrer Kindheit, an die Menschen, mit denen sie lebte, und an die Orte, an denen sie in ihren ersten zwanzig Lebensjahren verbrachte, um sich plastisch vorzustellen, wie diese Seiten im Jahr 1968 gelesen wurden. Was könnte ein junges ostdeutsches Mädchen aus dem Bild des Jungen, der Früchte von seinem Fahrradkarren verkauft (?) wohl machen? Und was ist mit den übrigen Informationen: „Wissenschaft, Technik, Kultur, Sport und Unterhaltung", die zwischen den Deckblättern lagen und zweifellos der Kulturpolitik des Regimes entsprachen und diese zum Ausdruck brachten?

Here, it seems to me that this is another tangled proposition on the relation between experience and endurance. I leave it to you, dear reader, to disentangle this one. I finish here, in medias res; we wait to see what will come next. ▬

1 Cf. the article "Happening", Art Terms, Tate, accessed 18 January 2020, https://www.tate.org.uk/art/art-terms/h/happening; and also Allan Kaprow, *Essays on the Blurring of Life and Art*, Jeff Kelley (ed.), Berkeley 1993.

2 Gayatri Spivak, *The Postcolonial Critic: Interviews, Strategies, Dialogues.* London 1990, pp. 62-3.

3 *Urania Universum* Band 14, Jena/Berlin, 1968, p. 480.

4 QuantenPhysik, 'Albert Einstein reads "The Common Language of Science" (Full version, 1941)', posted 16 April 2014, YouTube video, 8:45, https://www.youtube.com/watch?v=iEtQ-gQOBq8.

5 Jeff Kelley, "Acknowledgement", in: *Essays on the Blurring of Life and Art*, Jeff Kelley (ed.), Berkeley 1993, p. 82.

6 Allan Kaprow, "Manifesto", in: *Essays on the Blurring of Life and Art*, Jeff Kelley (ed.), Berkeley 1993, p. 82.

Die Wörter und Bilder, die 1968 zusammengetragen und als Jahrbuch veröffentlicht wurden, drückten das kollektive Leben einer bestimmten Zeit und eines bestimmten Ortes aus und überdauerte in Buchform bis ins Jahr 2018, in Antiquariaten verstaubend. Wie nimmt man dieses Buch im Jahr 2018 in Berlin wahr? Die Werkreihe, die die Arbeit *Urania Universum* konstituiert, bietet eine Proposition zum Verhältnis von Aushalten und Erfahrung als Antwort auf diese Frage. Die **Abb. 5** ist die Antwort von Katja Pudor auf diese Frage in Hinsicht auf Seite 480 des *Urania-Universum*-Bandes 14, die Sie auf **Abb. 6**. sehen. Die Künstlerin erlebt gelesene Wörter und hat diese Erfahrung ausgedrückt: Die Originalseite wurde in mehreren Schritten und mit mehreren Druckplatten überdruckt. Wir, die wir das Bild studieren, das einmal Seite 479 war, lesen nicht Wörter, sondern Farben – hellblau und schwarz und weiß, sich kreuzende Linien und die Formen, die sie erzeugen. Nur ein kleiner Teil des Originals ist noch erkennbar, als Hintergrund aus verblasstem rosa-braunen Papier von schlechter Qualität.

Welche Erfahrung machen wir, die wir jene, in diesem Prozess erzeugten Bilder lesen? Wir haben mehrere Optionen. Wir können unsere Erfahrung auf das Visuelle beschränken und währenddessen erkennen, dass unsichtbar unter den auf das Papier gedruckten Farbschichten Wörter verborgen sind, die einst für viele Menschen von Bedeutung waren. Oder wir schenken dem Prozess der Künstlerin besondere Aufmerksamkeit und ahmen ihre Erfahrung insofern nach, als wir uns die Zeit nehmen, die Worte auf der Rückseite des Bildes sorgfältig zu lesen. Wir könnten Seite 480 lesen und das Bild studieren, zu dem Seite 479 geworden ist.

Wenn wir uns mit dieser Arbeit befassen, können wir die Erfahrung des *Nicht-Aushaltens* machen. An die erste Option anknüpfend, haben wir die Möglichkeit, dieses Nicht-Aushalten als ein vages und komplettes Verschlüsseln zu erfahren. Die zweite Option, die wir uns eröffnen, indem wir uns Zeit nehmen, um „unsere Hausaufgaben zu machen", wie die Kulturtheoretikerin Gayatri Spivak[2] sagen würde, hilft uns, dieses vage Gefühl der Verschlüsselung „auszufüllen und es samt seiner seltsamen Details zu erleben. Beginnen wir mit dem Lesen auf Seite 480 oben. Wenn wir mit den jetzt unlesbaren Worten auf Seite 479 fortfahren, sind wir beim Thema Wissenschaft und Technologie in der Architektur im Jahr 1968. Der unbekannte Verfasser dieser Worte hat ein Zitat aus einem Vortrag verwendet, der 1941, mitten im Zweiten Weltkrieg, von Nobelpreisgewinner Albert Einstein gehalten wurde:

> *[...] neue Art, Wohnungen zu errichten, eine neue Art, Fabriken und Büros zu bauen und eine neue Vorstellung von Schönheit, die den Möglichkeiten der neuen Technik entsprach. Doch dann kam der zweite Weltkrieg und mit ihm der Zusammenbruch aller Vorstellung von einer Perfektionierung der kapitalistischen Welt durch die Technik. Einstein urteilte über diese kapitalistische Welt: ‚Höchste Perfektion der Mittel, höchste Konfusion der Ziele'.* [3]

Vielleicht kannten Leser*innen in der DDR 1968 dieses Zitat? Vielleicht war es damals allgemein bekannt, dass der berühmte Physiker jenen Vortrag, aus dem dieses Zitat stammt, mit der Zielsetzung beendete, die „einzig" richtige Methode zur Unterscheidung der sogenannten Gesetze der physischen Welt anzuwenden:

> *Selbst wenn nur ein kleiner Teil der Menschheit solche Ziele anstrebt, wird sich ihre Überlegenheit auf lange Sicht bewähren.*[4]

Woher kenne ich das Ende des Zitats am oberen Rand der Seite 480? Da wir weder das Jahr 1941 noch 1968 schreiben, googelte ich das Zitat und fand ein YouTube-Video von Einstein, der seine

Rede auf Englisch hielt. Während ich im Jahr 2019 der pompösen Prophezeiung Einsteins aus dem Jahr 1941 zuhörte und zusah, schrieb sich die Richtigkeit von Katja Pudors Kunst auf Seite 479 mit Nachdruck ein; mit einer wissenden verkörperten Gewissheit.

Zeitlich gesehen lenkt *Urania Universum* unseren Blick teilweise in die 1960er-Jahre zurück, ebenso wie eine im Werden begriffene Zeichnung, der ich bei meinem Besuch im Dezember 2018 im Berliner Atelier von Katja Pudor begegnet bin. Eine bestimmte Gruppe englischer Wörter, die in einer scheinbar endlosen Vielfalt von Handschriften mit vielen verschiedenen Zeichengeräten geschrieben worden war, erregte meine Aufmerksamkeit. Ich nutzte mein Telefon als Aufnahmegerät und las die Wörter, die ich identifizieren konnte, laut vor. Mithilfe dieser Aufnahme habe ich später den genauen Ursprung der Worte ermittelt, die laut Katja dem „Manifest von Allan Kaprow“ entsprechen. Die Worte ergeben das *Manifesto* (1966) des Erfinders der kalifornischen Kunst-Leben-Happenings der späten 1950er- und frühen 1960er-Jahre – ich finde sie auf Seite 82 eines Buches, das 1993 veröffentlicht wurde. Dieses Buch

> *[...] entstand aus einer retrospektiven „Ausstellung“ von Allan Kaprows Happenings [...] Trotz ihrer kunstweltlichen Infamie wurden die Happenings [...] nur von relativ wenigen besucht/erlebt. Aber [...] was als Werke der Avantgardekunst begonnen hatte, war bis 1966 [...] das Leben selbst geworden. Die Happenings wurden bald zu einer Art Mythologie [...] In der Hoffnung, sein Experiment mit den Bedeutungen des Alltagslebens zu verlängern, versöhnte sich Kaprow damit, das Genre der Avantgarde loszulassen*[5].

Mit dem Schreiben eines Manifests im Jahr 1966 versöhnte sich Kaprow offenbar mit seinem eigenen Ruhm als Künstler. Es folgt meine Auswahl der Absätze, die ich in Katjas abgeschriebenem Manifest identifizieren konnte.

> *What makes identifying oneself as an artist iconic is attestation ... to a philosophical stance before elusive alternatives of not-quite-art and not-quite life ...*
> *Although it is commonplace to bring such acts and thought to the gallery ... to do so blunts the power inherent in an arena of paradoxes...it evokes a history of cultural expectations that run counter to the poignant and absurd nature of art today ...*
> *... Contemporary artists are not out to supplant recent modern art with a better kind; they wonder what art might be. Art and life are not simply commingled; the identity of each is uncertain. To pose these questions in the form of acts that are neither and both artlike nor lifelike while locating them in the framed context of the conventional showplace is to suggest that there really are no uncertainties at all. The name on the gallery or stage door [or book cover] assures us that whatever is contained within is art, and everything else is life.*
> *[But] Precisely because art can be confused with life, it forces attention upon the aim of its ambiguities, to „reveal“ experience.* [6]

Und über das „Machen“ der Arbeit sagte Katja:

> *Für mich sind zwei Dinge wichtig. Während ich den Text wieder und wieder schreibe, verstehe ich mehr und mehr die Bedeutungen des Textes und denke, was der Text sagt. Und dann ist es die Textur dieses Textes auf dem Papier, wenn er mit der Hand geschrieben wird.*

Dies ist, so erscheint es mir, wieder ist eine verwickelte Proposition über die Beziehung zwischen Erfahrung und Aushalten. Ich überlasse es Ihnen, liebe*r Leser*in, diese zu entwirren. Ich beende meine Überlegungen hier, *in medias res*; mal sehen, was als nächstes kommt. ▬

1 Vgl. der Artikel „Happening“, Art Terms, Tate, abgerufen am 18. Januar 2020, https://www.tate.org.uk/art/art-terms/h/happening; sowie Allan Kaprow, *Essays on the Blurring of Life and Art*, hg. v. Jeff Kelley, Berkeley 1993, S. 82.

2 Gayatri Spivak. *The Postcolonial Critic: Interviews, Strategies, Dialogues*. London, S. 62–63.

3 *Urania Universum* Band 14, Jena / Berlin, 1968, S. 480.

4 QuantenPhysik, „Albert Einstein reads ‚The Common Language of Science‘ (Full version, 1941)“, hochgeladen am 16. April 2014, YouTube-Video, 8:45, https://www.youtube.com/watch?v= iEtQ-gQ0Bq8.

5 Jeff Kelley, „Acknowledgement“, in: *Essays on the Blurring of Life and Art*, hg. v. Jeff Kelley, Berkeley 1993, S. 82.

6 Allan Kaprow, „Manifesto“, in: *Essays on the Blurring of Life and Art*, hg. v. Jeff Kelley, Berkeley 1993, S. 82.

FUTURE PROOF

Collage, cut outs from
book pages and linol colour
on cardboard
2019

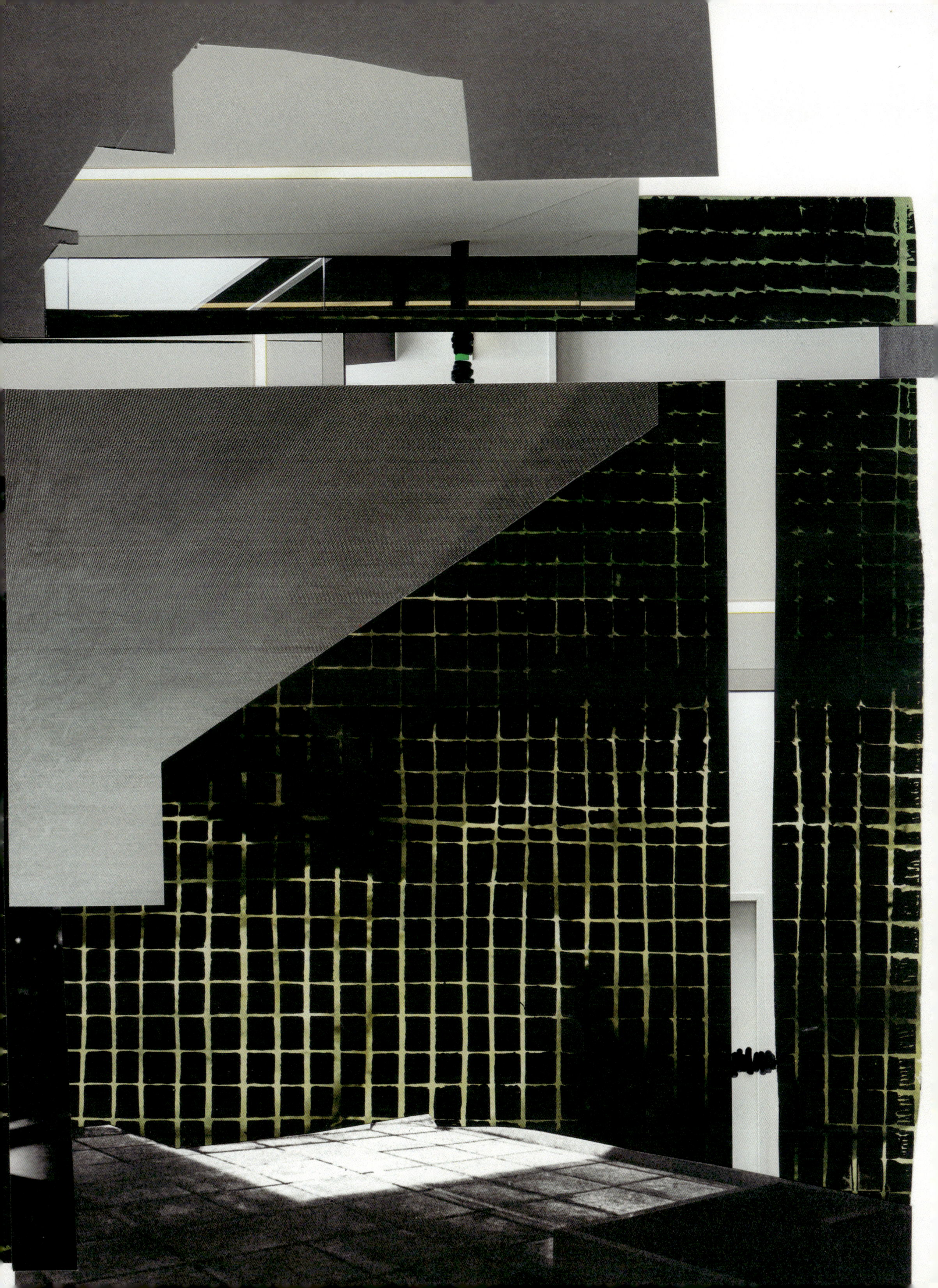

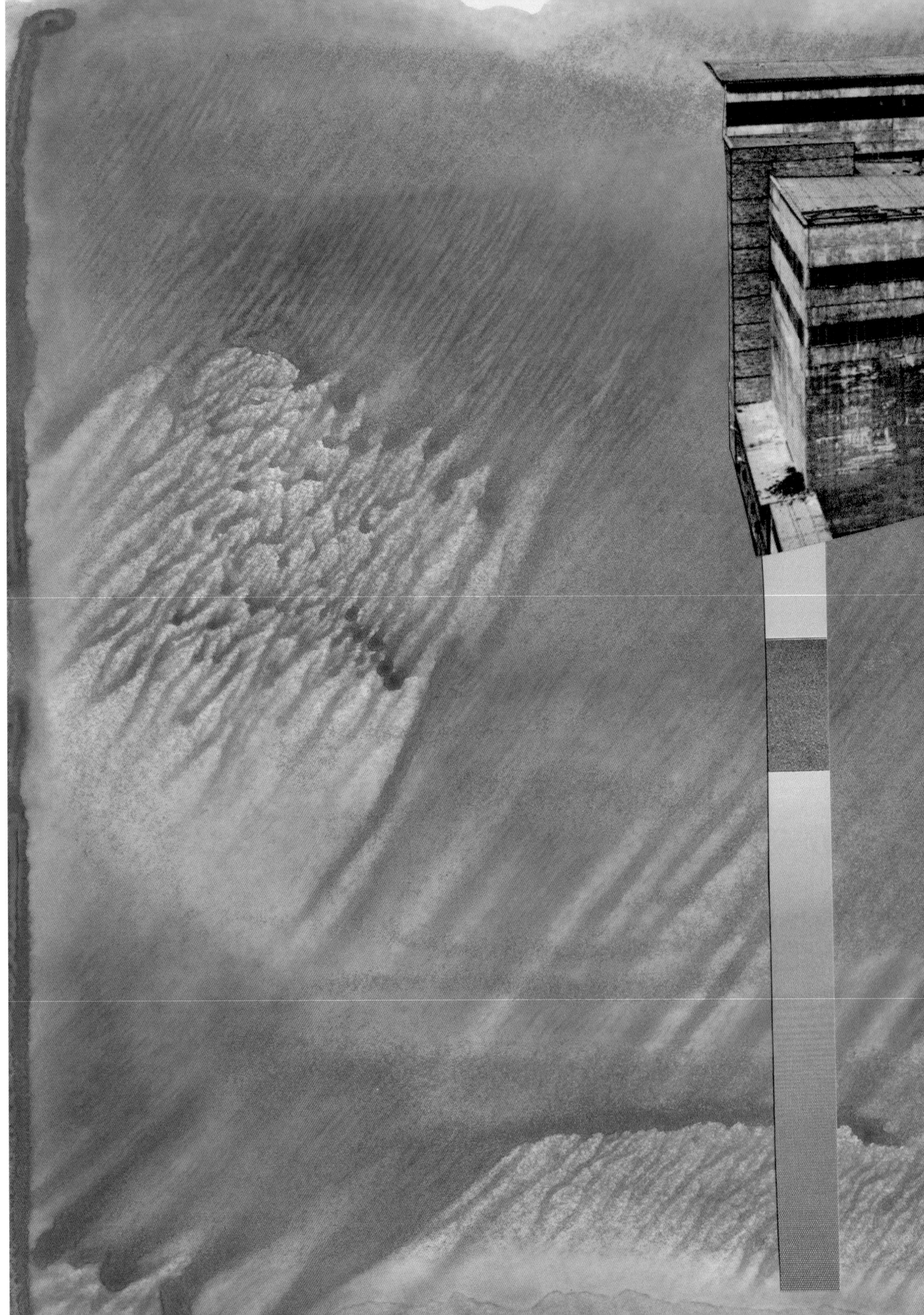

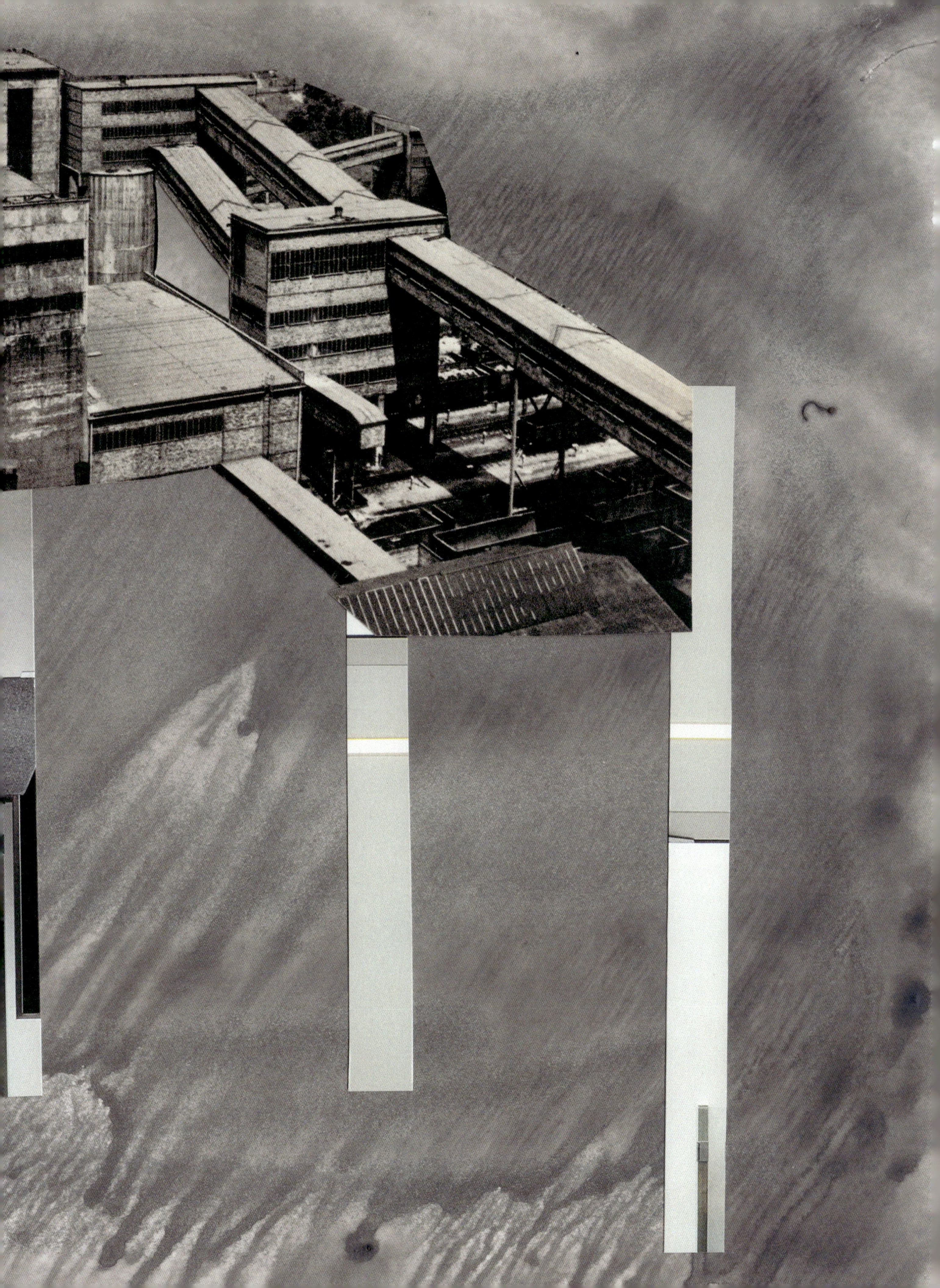

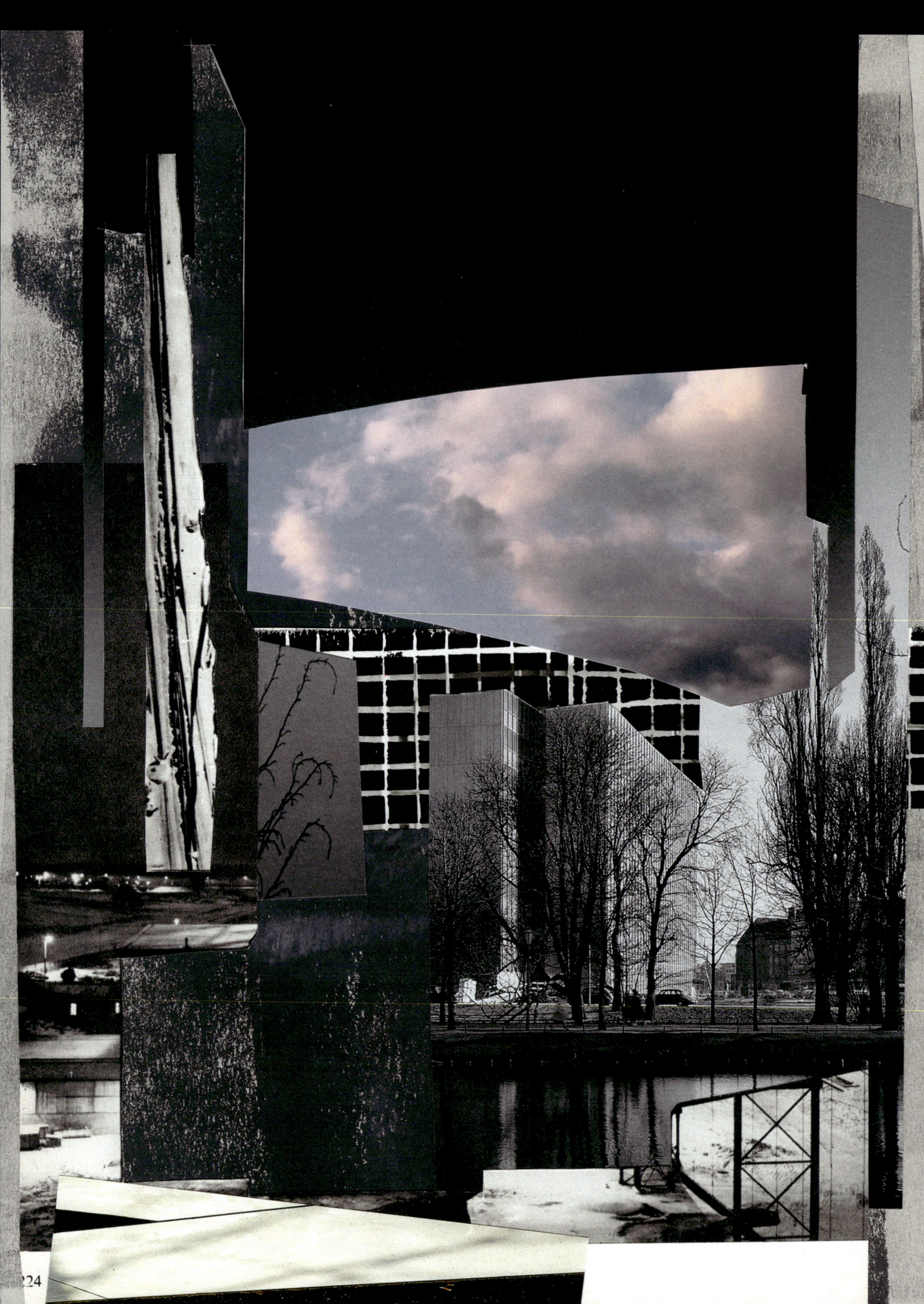

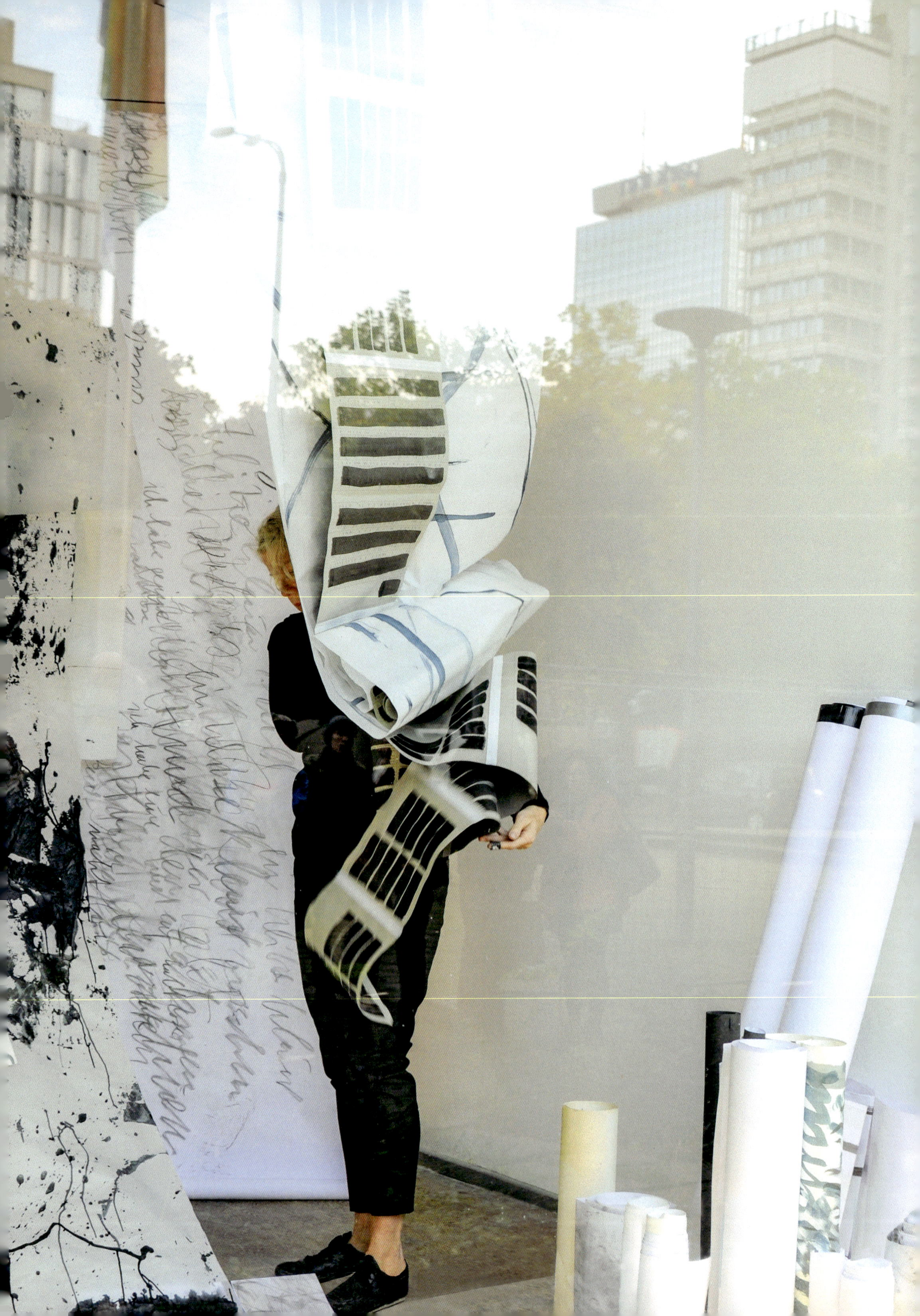

ANIPULATING THE ARCHIVE

Performance, duration: 30 min
Different materials on various papers
Haus der Statistik, Berlin
2019

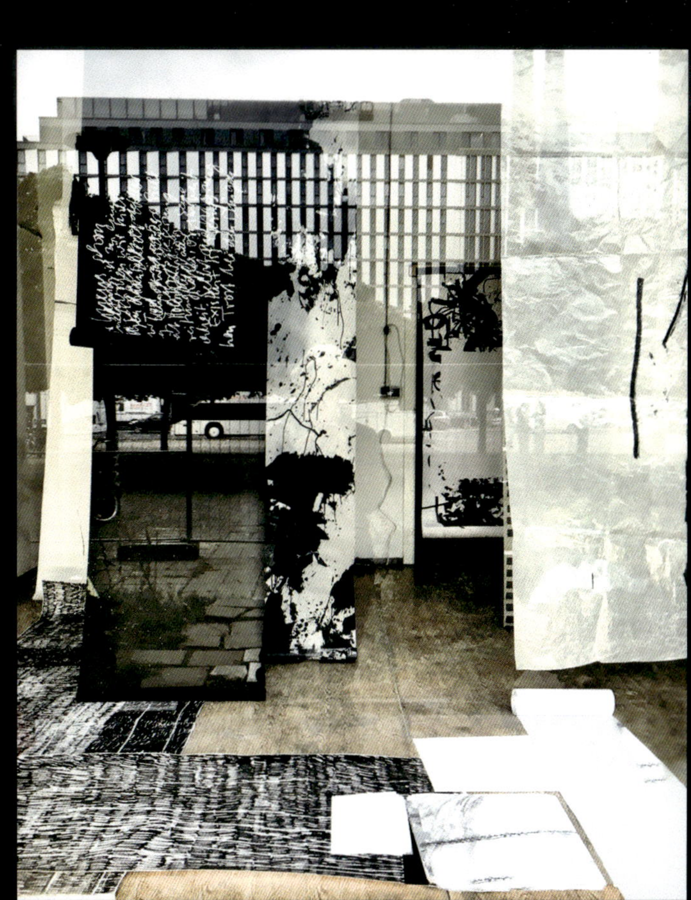

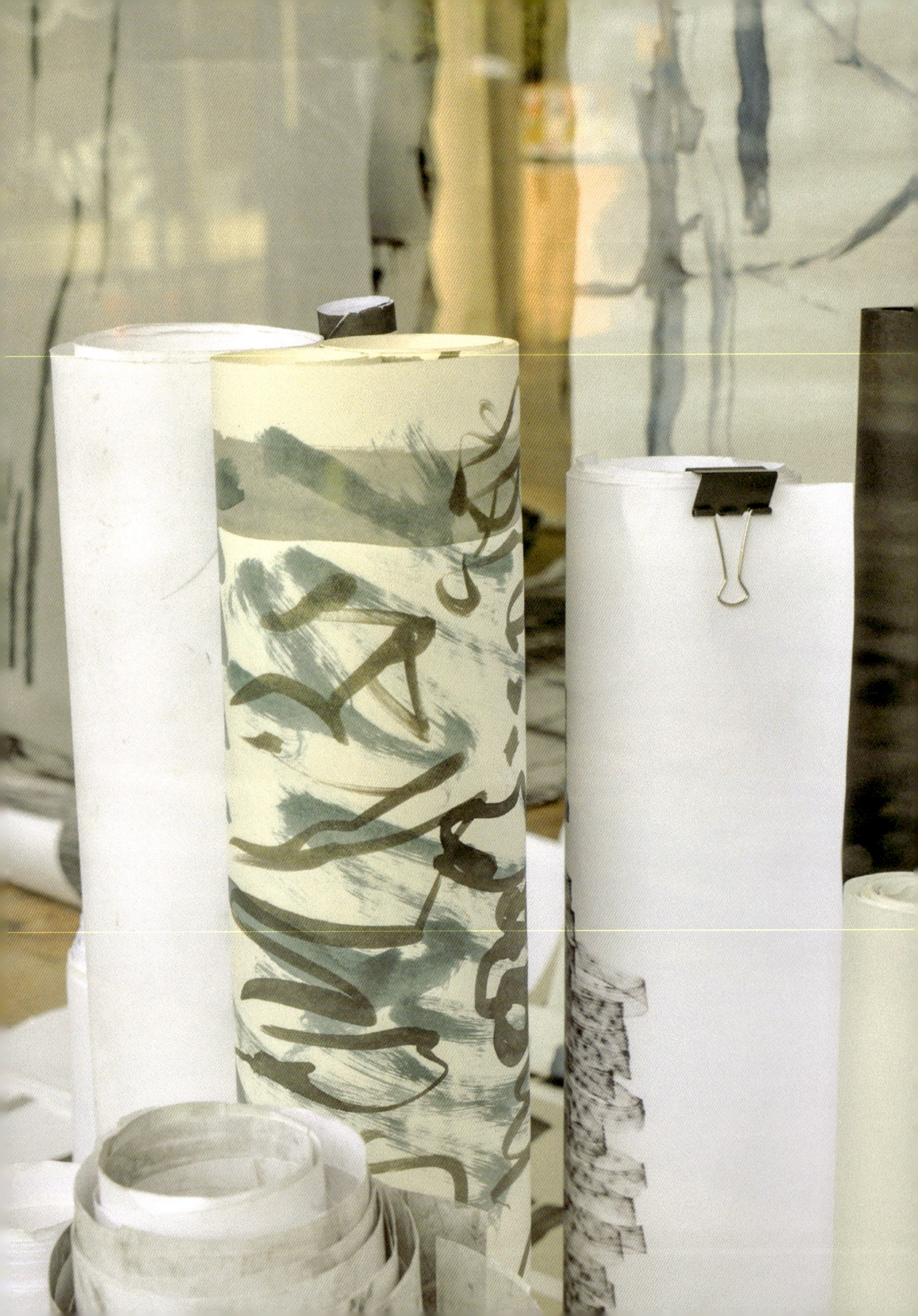

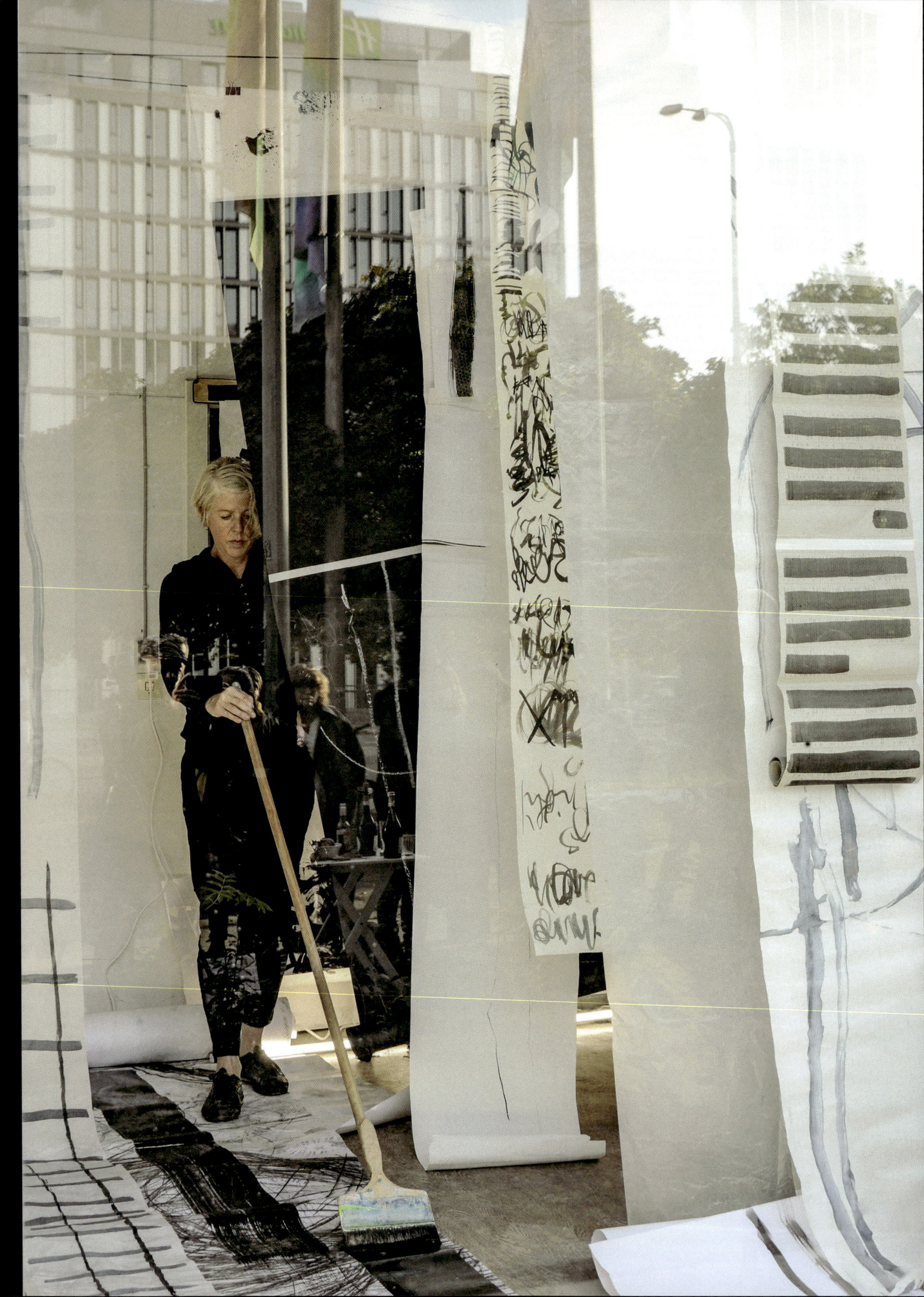

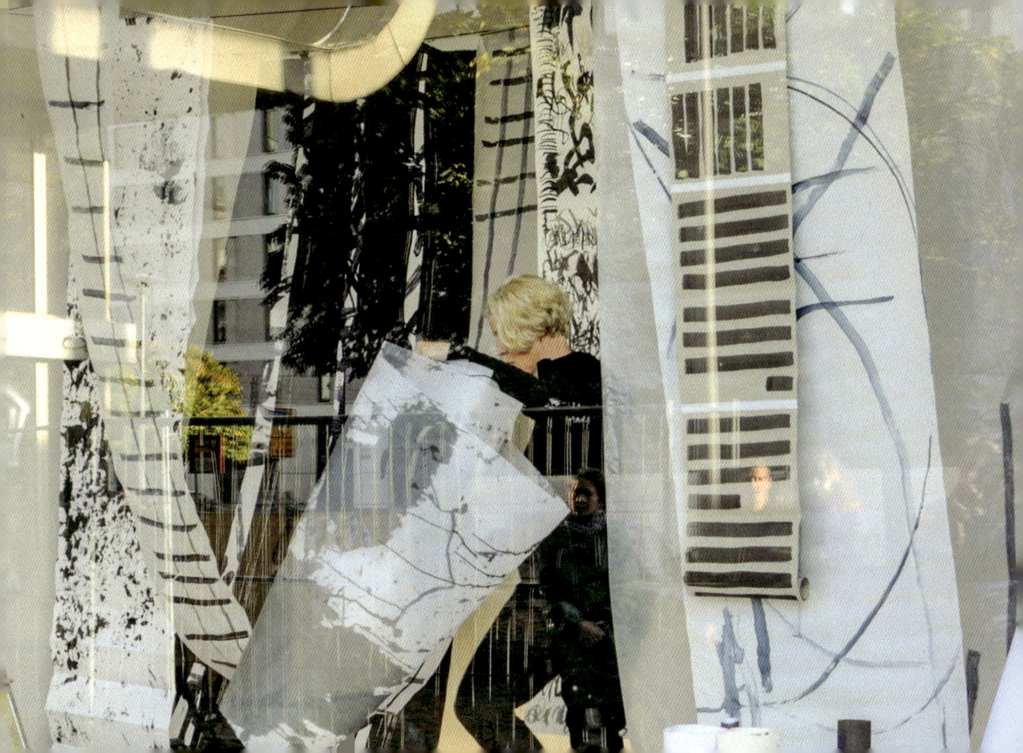

INDEX

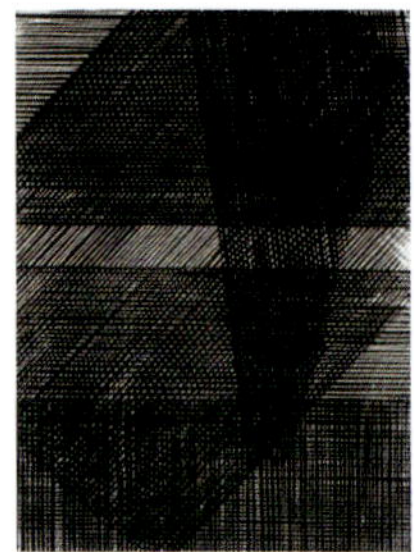

Clearance Space #11, 2019, multiple printing with one printing plate on fine art paper, 32 × 22 cm
Cover

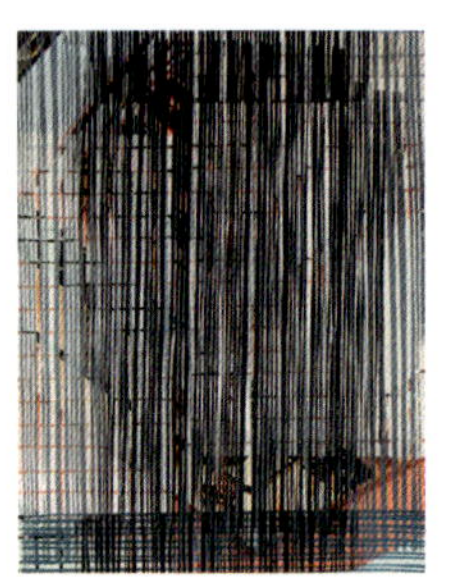

Protocols of Remembering #1, 2019, linocut from multiple plates on book page, 30,5×23 cm
Page 11

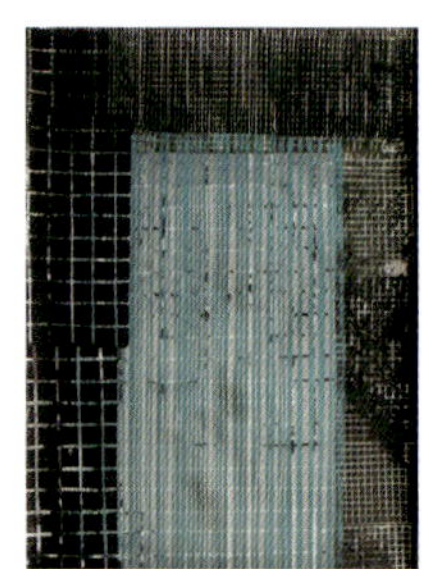

Protocols of Remembering #7, 2019, linocut from multiple plates on book page, 32,5 × 23,5 cm
Page 12

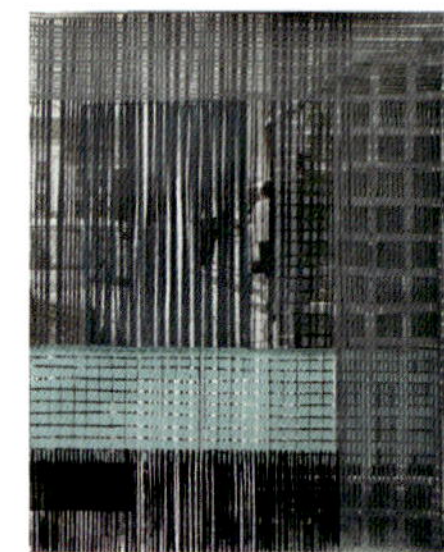

Protocols of Remembering #19, 2019, linocut from multiple plates on book page, 29,7 × 22,7 cm
Page 13

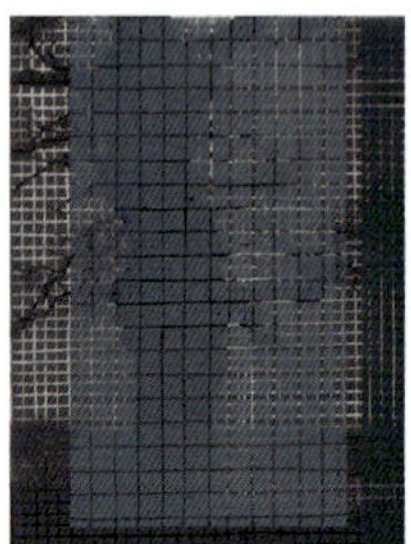

Protocols of Remembering #6, 2019, linocut from multiple plates on book page, 30 × 22,5 cm
Page 14

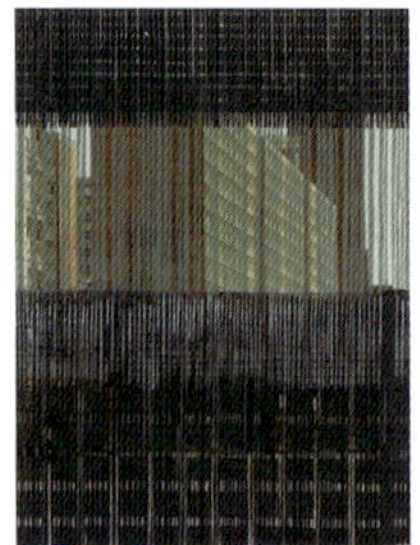

Protocols of Remembering #35, 2019, linocut from multiple plates on book page, 30 × 23 cm
Page 15

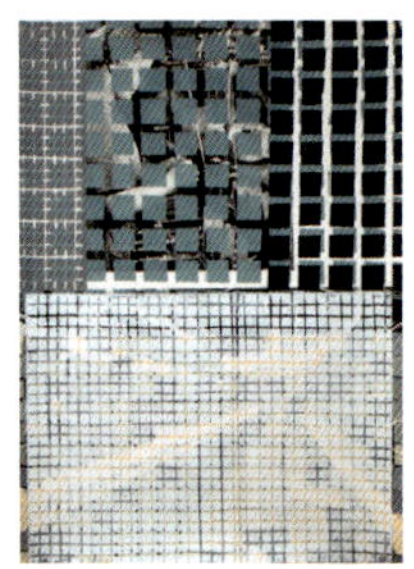

Protocols of Remembering #9, 2019, linocut from multiple plates on book page, 32,5 × 23,5 cm
Page 16

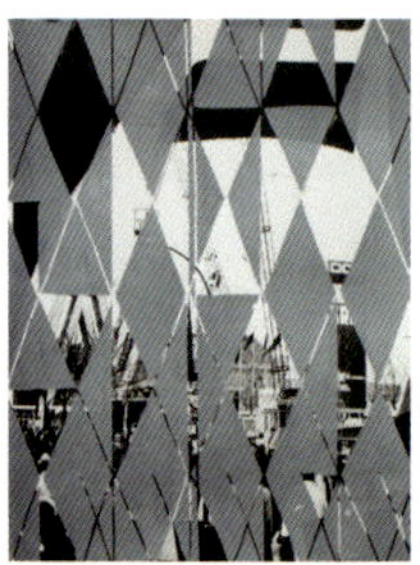

Protocols of Remembering #5, 2019, linocut from multiple plates on book page, 29,5 × 23 cm
Page 17

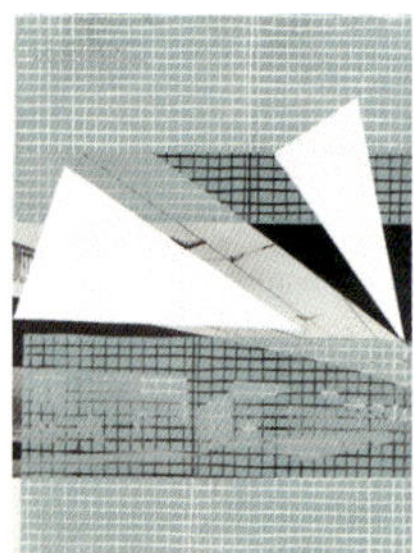

Protocols of Remembering #27, 2019, linocut from multiple plates on book page, 30 × 22,5 cm
Page 18

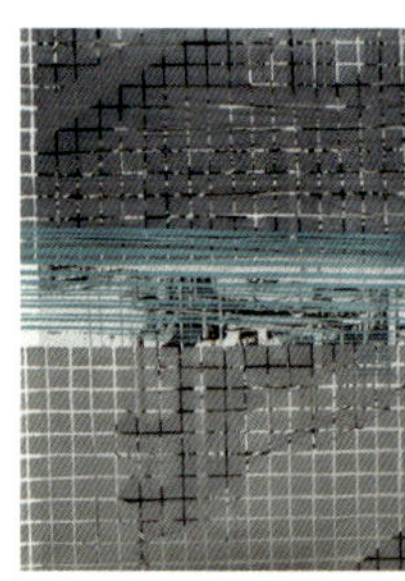

Protocols of Remembering #10, 2019, linocut from multiple plates on book page, 32,5 × 23,5 cm
Page 19

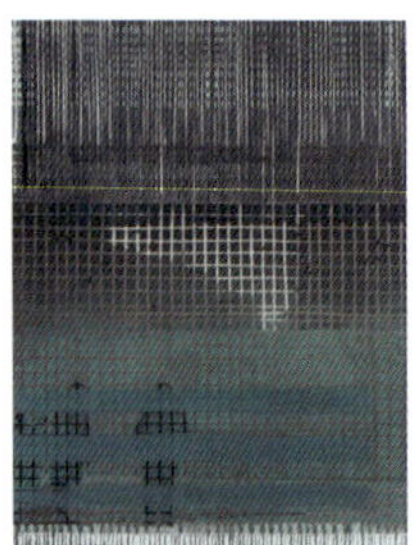

Protocols of Remembering #34, 2019, linocut from multiple plates on book page, 32,5 × 23 cm
Page 20

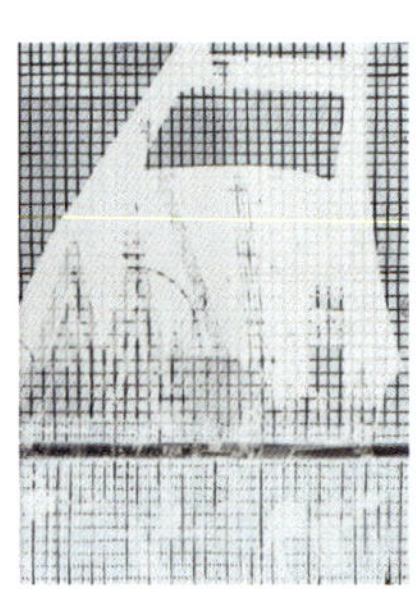

Protocols of Remembering #20, 2019, linocut from multiple plates on book page, 30 × 23 cm
Page 21

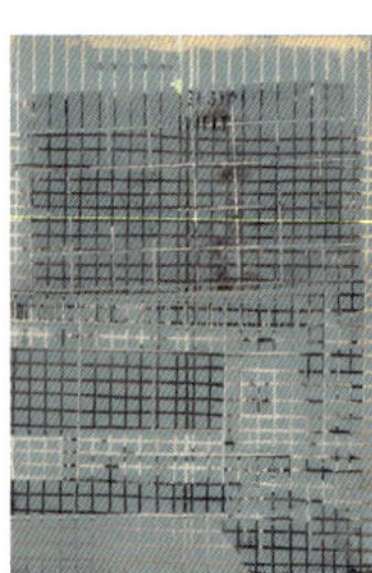

Urania Universum #25, 2018, linocut from multiple plates on book page, 23,5 × 15,5 cm
Page 29

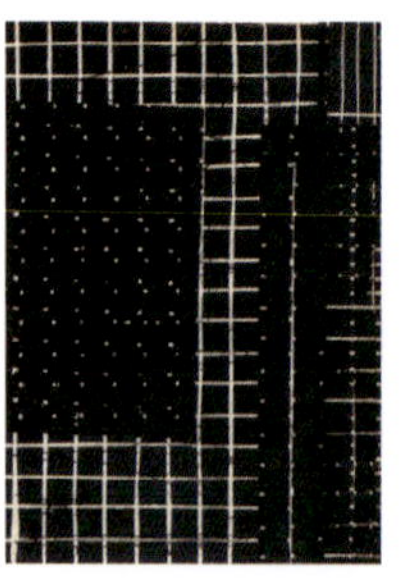

Urania Universum #99, 2018, linocut from multiple plates on book page, 23,5 × 15,5 cm
Page 30

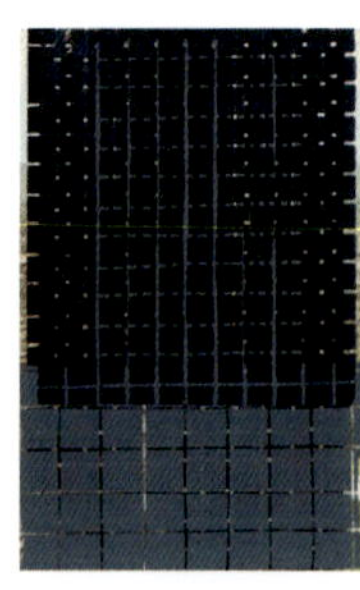

Urania Universum #13, 2018, linocut from multiple plates on book page, 23,5 × 15,5 cm
Page 31

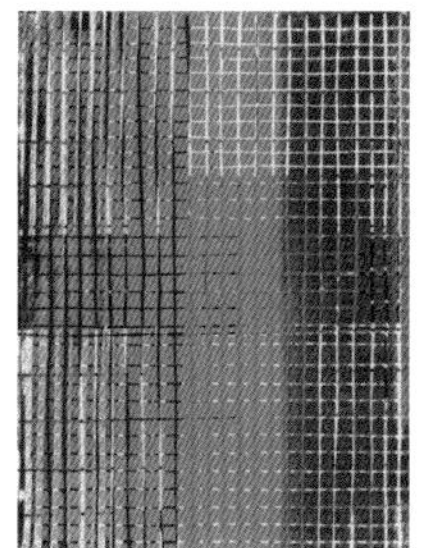

Urania Universum #5,
2018, linocut from
multiple plates on book
page, 21,5 × 15,5 cm

Page 32

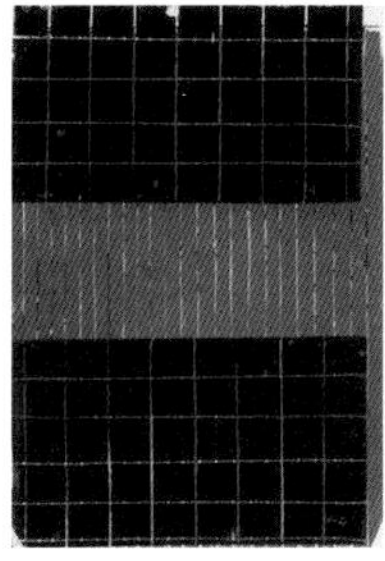

Urania Universum #7,
2018, linocut from
multiple plates on book
page, 23,5 × 15,5 cm

Page 33

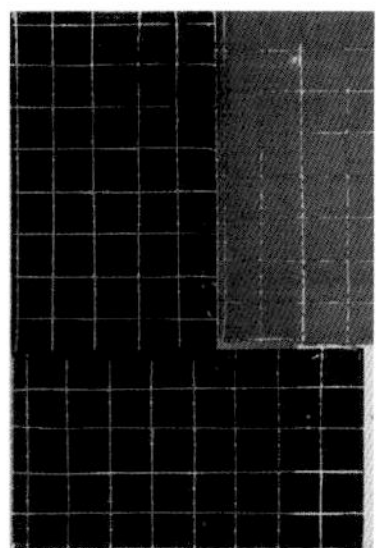

Urania Universum #17,
2018, linocut from
multiple plates on book
page, 23,5 × 15,5 cm

Page 34

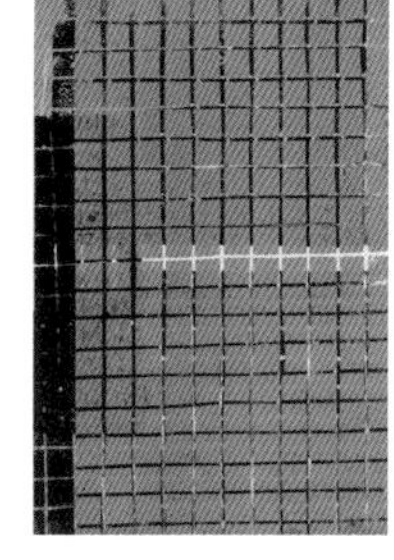

Urania Universum #1,
2018, linocut from
multiple plates on book
page, 23,5 × 15,5 cm

Page 35

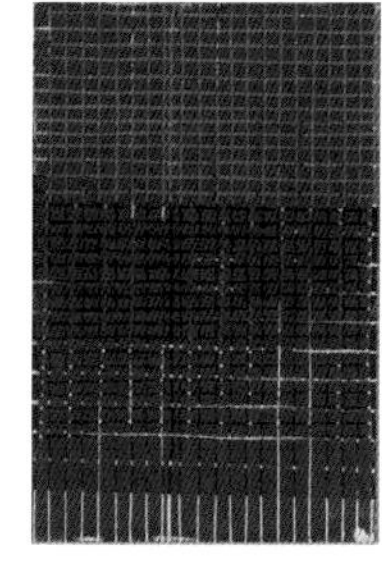

Urania Universum #57,
2018, linocut from
multiple plates on book
page, 23,5 × 15,5 cm

Page 36

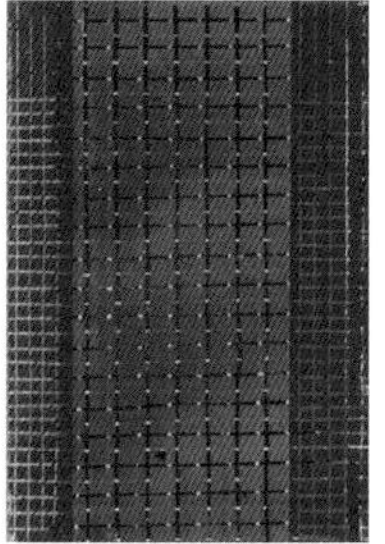

Urania Universum #37,
2018, linocut from
multiple plates on book
page, 23,5 × 15,5 cm

Page 37

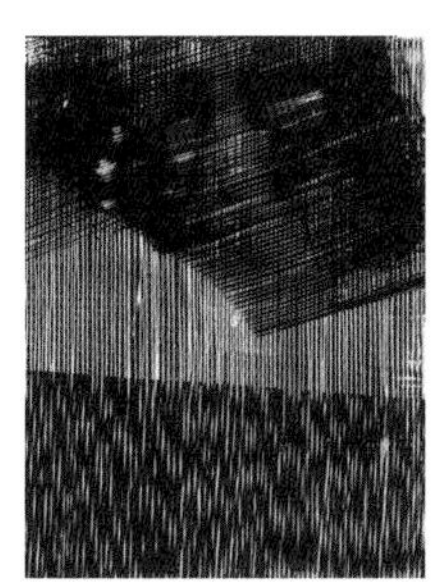

Clearance Space #12,
2019, linocut
from one plate on fine art
paper, 32 × 22 cm

Page 39

Clearance Space #1,
2019, linocut
from one plate on fine art
paper, 32 × 22 cm

Page 40

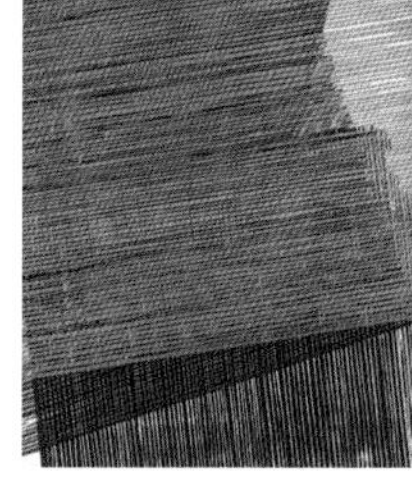

Clearance Space #10,
2019, linocut
from one plate on fine art
paper, 32 × 22 cm

Page 41

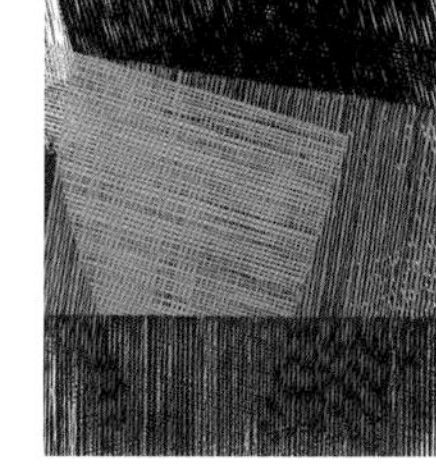

Clearance Space #4,
2019, linocut
from one plate on fine art
paper, 32 × 22 cm

Page 42

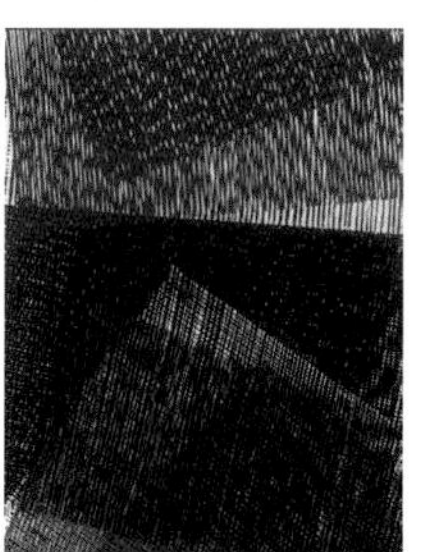

Clearance Space #5,
2019, linocut
from one plate on fine art
paper, 32 × 22 cm

Page 43

Clearance Space #14,
2019, linocut
from one plate on fine art
paper, 32 × 22 cm

Page 44

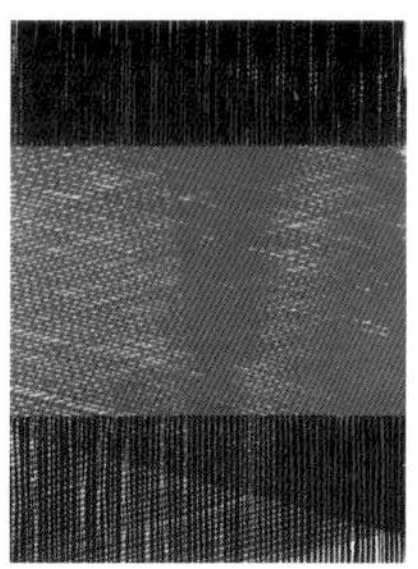

Clearance Space #15,
2019, linocut
from one plate on fine art
paper, 32 × 22 cm

Page 45

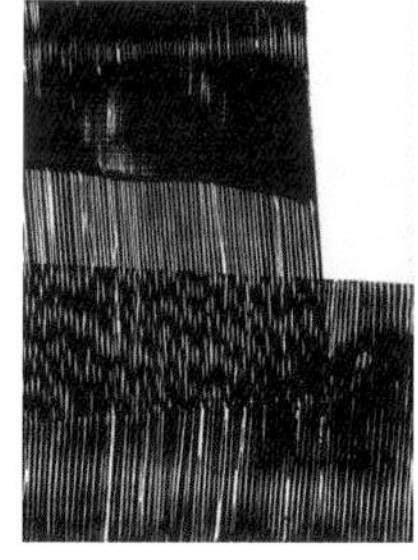

Clearance Space #13,
2019, linocut
from one plate on fine art
paper, 32 × 22 cm

Page 46

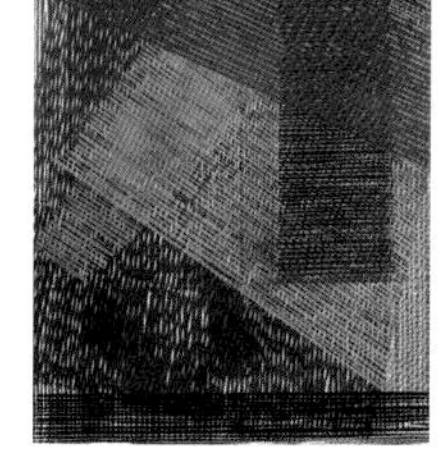

Clearance Space #3,
2019, linocut
from one plate on fine art
paper, 32 × 22 cm

Page 47

*Writing.
A Manifesto #2*,
2018, ink on paper,
100 cm x 70 cm

Page 60

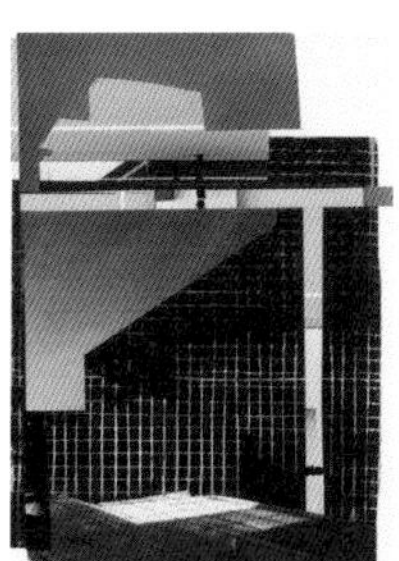

Future Proof #18, 2019,
collage, cut outs
from book pages and linol
colour on cardboard,
29 cm x 21 cm

Page 65

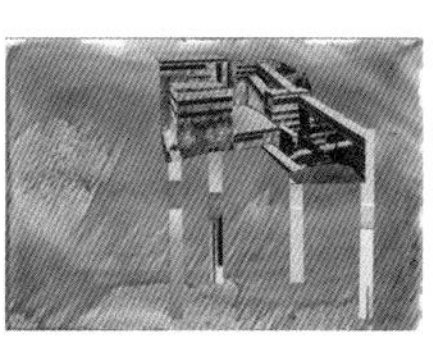

Future Proof #15, 2019,
collage, cut outs
from book pages and linol
colour on paper,
21 cm x 29 cm,

Pages 66–67

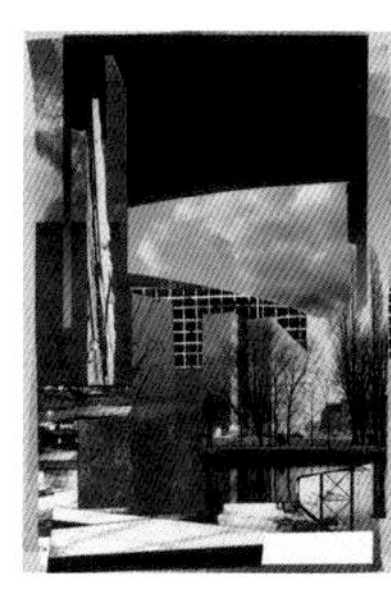

Future Proof #19, 2019,
collage, cut outs
from book pages and linol
colour on cardboard,
29 cm x 21 cm,

Page 68

ABOUT THE ARTIST AND THE AUTHORS

Katja Pudor is an artist based in Berlin. She studied fine arts and painting at the Kunsthochschule Weißensee Berlin and completed her education in the master's program in 2005. She has received numerous grants and scholarships, including the Visual Arts Residency Grant, Schloß Wiepersdorf; Artist's Grant of the Ministry of Science, Research, and Culture of the State of Brandenburg in 2016; and the Artist's Grant of the Berlin Senate Department for Culture and Europe in 2009. She initiated several cooperative projects, including the Projektraum Stedefreund, Berlin (2006-2013). Her works have been shown internationally in numerous exhibitions. Katja Pudor focuses on the process of developing an artistic work and visualizes the phases of experimentation and invention. She addresses these as a form of social space and relates them to physical places, different temporal planes, and materials such as paper, fabric, charcoal, and ink. Drawing works as a form of mediation. Pudor constantly expands, rearranges, and rewrites her own drawing-based archive in site-specific installations and performances. These experimental arrangements are to be understood as inquiries into the "recent past" and as an attempt to make past and present visible at the same time. Through the layering in the drawings, various sediments of memory, meaning, and reference are uncovered in the sense of an archaeology of the present and transferred into new contexts of meaning.

Thank you for this special form of collaborative work:

Birgit Effinger lives and works as an independent curator and lecturer in Berlin. She supports artists, designers, and film-makers in the development of their professional careers with coaching, advice, workshops, and courses at various European art schools. Since 2017 she has been the director of see up – zentrum für Abolvent*innen, an offer tailored to students and graduates of all faculties at the weissensee art academy in Berlin. From 2002 to 2018 she was project manager of the Goldrausch Künstlerinnenprojekt, a professional one-year training programme for women artists. Birgit Effinger writes regularly articles for art magazines and catalogues; her main topics are professionalism in art and culture, aesthetics and politics, and discourses in contemporary art.

Helen Verran is one of the most innovative social philosophers of our times; she is based near Melbourne, Australia. Verran worked at the University of Melbourne for 25 years and was the recipient of various fellowships on all seven continents. Since the 1980s, inspired by working with Aboriginal Australians and in Nigeria, she has been developing the novel empirical epistemology 'Relational Empiricism'. She wrote extensively about this in her book „Science and African Logic" (Chicago Press, 2001), which won the Ludwik Fleck Prize. Currently, she is working on the ethnography of the history of concepts in social and other sciences, in arts, policy making (particularly environmental policy), and, most relevantly, in collectively shared everyday routines.

Josefine Raasch is a social anthropologist with an interest in knowledge production. She has studied European Ethnology and Education at the Humboldt University Berlin and received her PhD in Science and Technology Studies from Swinburne University of Technology in Melbourne. She has worked with Helen Verran and her relational empiricism since 2011, has translated and written about Verran's concepts, and taught them at Ruhr University Bochum, University of Vienna, and Humboldt University Berlin.

Catrin Sonnabend works as a freelance graphic designer and art director in Berlin, focusing on editorial, catalogue and book design. She works for and with clients from the publishing industry, art, culture and lifestyle. She is co-founder and organizer of the designer network Format Club.

And special thanks for her special views and the photos of all my performances:
Silke Schneider

COLOPHON

CONCEPT

Katja Pudor / Catrin Sonnabend

DESIGN

Catrin Sonnabend

TEXTS

Birgit Effinger
Helen Verran

TRANSLATION

Brian Currid pp. 22–27;
Patrick Hubenthal and
Josefine Raasch pp. 54–63

COPY EDITING

DISTANZ Verlag and
Andrea Scrima

PHOTO CREDITS

Silke Schneider
pp. 3, 5, 8, 9, 72, 74–77

PRINTING

Ruksaldruck GmbH & Co. KG,
Berlin

DISTRIBUTION

edel Germany GmbH
www.edel.com
international-books@edel.com

ISBN 978-3-95476-315-3
Printed in Germany

PUBLISHED BY

DISTANZ Verlag
www.distanz.de